Listen to Us, We're Not That Stupid

The people's prescription for what
REALLY ails America's health care system

By
John E. Skvarla III
with
Frank Elliott

D1367463

Library of Congress Cataloging-in-Publication Data

Skvarla, John E., 1948-
    Listen to us, we're not that stupid : the people's prescription
for what really ails America's health care system / John E.
Skvarla with Frank M. Elliott.
        p.226 6x9 in
    Includes bibliographic references.
    ISBN 0-930095-28-6 : $16.95. — ISBN 0-930095-29-4 (pbk.) :
$12.00
        1. Medical care—United States. 2. Medical care—United
States—History. 3. Health care reform—United States. I. Elliott,
Frank M. II. Title.
RA395.A3S567 1994
362.1'0973—dc20

Dedicated To
Elizabeth, Matt, Kate and Chelsea

Great appreciation also
to Leisa Wolfe, who graciously endured
the "1000" redrafts and to my parents for their
values and support.

Listen to Us, We're Not That Stupid

TABLE OF CONTENTS

Section 3. How Do We Get Out?

Epilogue: It's As Easy As One - Two - Three

Selected Bibliography

WHAT ARE THE FACTS?

a. In 1992, how much did the U.S. government collect in taxes?

b. In 1991, how much did the U.S. spend on Defense?

c. In 1992, how much did the U.S. spend on Education?

d. In 1992, how much did the U.S. spend on Health Care?

e. In 1991, what ailment had the highest amount of health care spending?

f. In 1991, what ailment had the second highest amount of health care spending?

g. In 1991, what ailment had the most number of patient visits?

h. In 1991, what ailment had the second highest number of patient visits?

i. In 1991, what business sectors spent more as a percent of the GDP than health care?

j. In 1991, what business sector had the greatest percentage increase for not providing health insurance to their employees?

k. What was the percent increase?

l. In 1991, what business sector had the highest per capita spending?

m. In 1991, how much was the per capita spending on health care in the U.S.?

n. In 1991, what has the second highest business sector for per capita spending in the U.S.?

o. In 1991, how much was the per capita spending for this second highest sector?

p. In 1980, employee health care costs equaled what percent of corporate profits?

q. In 1990, employee health care costs equaled what percent of corporate profits?

Answers:
a. $1.2 Trillion
b. $375 Billion
c. $441 Billion
d. $850 Billion
e. Heart Disease
f. Low Back Pain
g. Upper Respiratory Ailment (The Common Cold)
h. Low Back Pain (est. 400 million)
i. None. Federal Government Spending—25%;
     Health care —13%
j. Doctors' Offices
k. 29%
l. Health Care
m. $3,160 per person
n. Legal expenses
o. $300 per person
p. 24%
q. 100%   The amount spent on health care roughly
     equaled all corporate profits. If corporations
     had not had health care costs, they would have
     doubled their profits.

"There is an important difference between "customers" and patients. As customers we shop and bargain and evaluate. As patients and potential patients we are heavily influenced by our own fears of illness and by the experts in the white coats."

Dr. Rashi Fein,
Professor of Medical Economics
Harvard University

FOREWORD

This book was born of frustration and ignorance. Naively, I once believed that any company delivering products that offered better quality, reduced costs, and gave its customers a competitive advantage had a clear opportunity for success in a free enterprise system. Build a better mousetrap and the world will beat a path to your door, right? Our mousetrap was a machine called the B-200 that gave health care providers the first objective and functional means for diagnosing and treating low-back injuries. Low-back pain is a medical monster. Eighty percent of all Americans suffer from this affliction. After heart disease, American society spends more money treating this injury than any other ailment. In 1991, the total was $60 billion — yes, BILLION. And, aside from the common cold, Americans go to the doctor more for low back pain than for any other complaint. Our technology provided a revolution in how to treat what is both the nation's second most common medical problem, and its second most expensive medical problem. Without this technology, trying to diagnose a low-back ailment is, in the words of one physician, like trying to explore a cave without a flashlight. Obviously, there was a market for this device. With great expectations our company began marketing this better mousetrap. Some of the world instantly beat a path to our door. In 1989 and 1990 alone, more than thirteen major publications, including *Fortune, Business Week,* and *The Wall*

Street Journal, wrote about the revolution in diagnosis as the result of the B-200. Mainstream business publications like *Fortune* knew that their readers would be interested because American businesses — especially manufacturers — knew only too well the cost to them of low back problems. Corporate America considers low-back pain its number one health problem. Of course, the device also caught the attention of professional journals such as *Occupational Health and Safety* and *Modern Healthcare,* just to name two. Over one hundred scholarly articles have also been published about the merits of this technology.

There are more than 100,000 health care providers in the United States who treat low-back problems — doctors, physical therapists, chiropractors, acupuncturists, osteopaths, massage therapists, and a growing number of other kinds of therapists. The market for the B-200 was enormous. Fortunately, our company quickly became the world leader in the development of computer-assisted diagnostic and rehabilitation technology for this ailment. Our corporate mission was quite simple: to increase the quality of care to patients; to reduce societal costs for low-backs; and to distinguish our customers as being the best in the business by enabling them to accomplish the first two goals. Almost 1,000 health care providers around the world have in fact adopted this new and more efficient level of health care. But all the good press and the number one position in the world didn't bring the explosive growth that the demographics and statistics predicted. When I finally figured out why medical providers were so hard to convince, I began to see our health care system for what it is: an amazingly ingenious economic system. If you're intelligent enough to get into a medical school, if you pay your dues and are willing to spend a few years of apprenticeship, our medical system can make you more than comfortably rich. And our device, to a great extent, threatened this comfortable existence.

Why? Put yourself in the shoes of a provider. You may be the best (or the worst) practitioner in the world, and now some upstart company (headed by a non-physician) is telling you how to do your job better and more effectively. Telling you that if you want to succeed in the long run, the components of quality and cost effectiveness must be integral to the patterns of your practice. Moreover, you probably won't look kindly on some invention that might make you accountable to your patients. This is generally an uncomfortable arrangement for practitioners who for years now have had absolute control over the patient-professional interplay. We've all heard the lines: "Trust me, I'm your doctor." And, "Don't worry, insurance will pay for it." This control by physicians gets to the heart of the perceived threat posed by the B-200, and to the heart of why our health care costs are out of control.

If you are involved in the extraordinarily lucrative niche of treating muscular injuries of the lower back, why would you want the system to change? Without the new technology, these injuries are entirely subjective. "Tell me if it hurts." Your patients enter a twilight zone of physical diagnosis and rehabilitation from which there is no exit. They're in a totally subjective environment for which surgery is too often the ultimate noncure. How could you possibly welcome a new technology that requires new knowledge, genuine accountability, and could very well threaten your income?

This is not to vilify health care providers. They're simply human beings acting rationally under the ground rules the system has created. Through decades of happenstance, we have created a medical system that gives everyone — doctors, patients, insurance companies, drug companies, and even medical-technology companies — the wrong motivations. Left to itself, our medical system is designed to lead automatically to continuously escalating expenditures and costs. That is exactly what is happening in our system today, and why we now are facing a crisis in health care.

Uwe Reinhardt, the James Madison Professor of Political Economics at Princeton University, recently commented that our health care system resembles the end result of a party game in which drunken revelers purposely attempt to design the most screwed-up system possible. Ours is a health care system that has excluded more than 37 million U.S. citizens — more than half of them full-time workers or their dependents — who do not have health insurance because neither they nor their employer can afford it. But in reality these people don't go without medical care. They show up in a hospital emergency room, at a stage when their ailment will cost far more to treat than at an earlier stage. They show up at a time when the cost of their care is simply passed on to those that can pay. And here's the shocker: The worst offender in skipping out on these payments is the federal government. The government does not pay the full cost of caring for the tens of millions of people on Medicare and Medicaid. The cost of treating the indigent and the elderly is passed on to those who do pay. In 1991, for every dollar billed to a private patient, 32 cents was to cover the cost of caring for the indigent and elderly through government programs. At the rate things are going, this number will be 50 cents on the dollar by 1995. So don't think for a minute that by allowing so many millions to go without medical insurance we have lowered the cost of medical care in the United States. Just the opposite. We spend far more per person on health care than any other country in the world — an astounding $3,160 per person in 1991. Yet, with the exception of South Africa, we are the only industrialized nation that does not provide for the health care of all its citizens. So we are spending more but getting less. Clearly, our country needs to devise a national health care system before the cost of staying healthy bankrupts our society. The only way to know how to change a system is to know how it works. This nation is embarking on a great debate over how to change the existing health care system, and through special interest groups, lobbyists, and "spin doctors," the people who either control or want to control the system are laboring to frame the debate. If this debate is left to the providers and the insurance industry, the chief causes of our spiraling health bill will never even be addressed. If they had their way, of course, they would keep the system we have — it's far too lucrative to change. If we leave it to the politicians, 14% of our domestic economy will soon be under the control of the federal government.

The individuals and the corporations in the U.S. can no longer stand the economic pain from a health care system so artfully yet ignorantly created. So now our society has come to accept the fact that reform is inevitable. And every special interest group and politician is hoping to mold reform to suit their purposes. This book is to help the rest of us see what the system is about before we get saddled with "reform" that helps no one and might well make matters worse. This book is for all those people who believe that the free market principals of quality and cost-effectiveness should be legitimate components of our health care system, but who are currently paying the price for the "inebriated planners."

John E. Skvarla III
January, 1994

Section 1:

What Have We Got?

SO WHAT ARE THE FACTS?

a. Where does the U.S. rank internationally in health of its population?

b. In 1942, how much did an appendectomy (with a 6-day hospital stay) cost?

c. In 1992, how much did an appendectomy (with a 3-day hospital stay) cost?

d. Between 1942 and 1992, how much did the appendectomy cost go up?

e. What was the national average income in 1992?

f. What was the average salary of medical residents in 1992?

Answers:
a. 15th
b. $31.49
c. $5,429.60
d. 17,000%
e. About $14,500
f. About $36,000

CHAPTER 1:
HOW SMART DO YOU
HAVE TO BE?
A FABLE

Let's suppose that you are given a fresh start in business. No longer do you have to worry about selling your product, generating new business, developing new products, keeping your customers happy, collecting for sales, spending less than you collect, managing people and doing all those other things which shorten your life considerably.

Your fresh start comes with some minor strings attached. You can't begin to actually work for yourself until you are at least 30 years old. Between the ages of 25 and 30 you must serve an apprenticeship. However, during this apprenticeship you will be paid a salary considerably above the national average.

Your new profession is in the restaurant business. It's a good business to be in. People must eat, so there will always be a need for your service and the products you provide.

Now, the goals of your restaurant are quite simple; to provide good food and make as much money as possible. These are realistic goals, and totally in keeping with the laws of human nature. How smart do you have to be succeed?

Before I answer this question, let's look at the rules of the game:

Rule Number One: As a result of serving your apprenticeship, you received a specialty license for this restaurant, so not just anyone can compete with you.

Rule Number Two: In this restaurant, there are no prices on the menus.

Rule Number Three: Since you are trained as a professional restauranteur, after asking a few questions, such as, "How hungry are you?" or, "What did you have for breakfast?" YOU alone determine what the customers will have to eat.

But wait, you say. The customers will never stand for this. You might order something that the customer can't afford or doesn't like. Isn't the customer going to demand to know what all this is costing?

No. Because there is...

Rule Number Four: The customer doesn't pay the bill. Like all the other restaurants in town, the bill is sent to an insurance company for payment. Moreover, the customer doesn't even have to pay for the insurance coverage. The customer's employer does. So the customer could care less about how much food is ordered by you or how much it costs. All the customer knows is that he has a great appetite to satisfy and only the best will do. Why not the $500 bottle of wine? If the wine isn't finished or food is left on the table, so what? It really doesn't matter. From the customer's perspective, he isn't paying for it. And, if satisfying the customer's voracious appetite requires turning the process over to a food specialist, what does it matter? As long as the customer gets the desired results and the process doesn't cost him anything, who cares? For all the customer knows, the restaurant owner could be submitting falsified invoices for food not actually served. Who cares? Not the customer — someone else is paying the bill. Let someone else worry about it. That's a problem for the insurance company.

Finally, Rule Number Five: The insurance company does not act as the middleman for free. As its compensation, it gets to keep a percentage of the premiums paid by the customer's employer for the coverage. Every year the restaurant's price hikes are simply passed on to the good ol' guy who signs the paychecks — the employer — in the form of increased insurance premiums.

Under this system, you and every other restaurant owner will want all of your patrons to have three, four or five course meals, because that increases the bill and hence, your income. More is clearly better.

Under this system, the customers quickly learn to expect the very best. Give me the finest filet mignon. Give me two filets! And if after the main course everyone is full but they would like a little taste of that chocolate cheesecake on the dessert cart, of course you'll insist that they take the whole piece. And even if they only want a bite, they'll agree. Who cares?

As for the insurance company? Well, as long as they can pass the cost of this feeding frenzy to the employer, they don't mind the waste. After all, the insurance company is paid as a percentage of the bill, so the higher the bill, the higher THEIR income. It's a wonderful system. Everybody gets something without paying anything.

Of course such a system is so laughable, and so implausible, as to be ridiculous. Anyone can see that it is tailor-made to give everyone the wrong incentives — incentives that foster wastefulness and ever-higher costs.

But this is how we provide health care in the United States.

The founders of the now-defunct Soviet Union implemented what in theory was the most enlightened, and most compassionate, system of government yet devised. No one would go wanting. Everyone would receive according to their needs. There was just one problem: It was contrary to human nature. We humans, with very few exceptions, invariably take the path of least resistance. Under communism, the path of least resistance led to working less and producing less. That's because everyone's needs were to be met regardless of what they produced. Working harder would not necessarily get you ahead. Over time, the standard of living in the Soviet Union — even by such essential measures as the production of food — collapsed because there was very little motivation to produce. The system did not have the right incentives.

Likewise, our health care system is bankrupting society because it too is running counter to human nature. And we too are losing. Health care costs in the United States are increasing at more than three times the rate of inflation, because we lack the incentives to control costs. In fact, the incentives are just the opposite, to drive costs higher and higher.

Health care providers are paid when they perform procedures operations, tests, and so forth. The more they do, the more they are paid. Patients, who are shielded from the costs, have no reason to quibble about number of procedures or the price, and in fact, usually demand the most and the best regardless of a cost they don't even know. And as we saw in our restaurant, insurance companies, until recently, also had no reason to worry about cost. Insurance industry profits may only average 1.74 percent of premiums, but what would you rather have, 1.74 percent of a million dollars or 1.74 percent of a billion dollars? In effect, the insurance industry sold its corporate customers down the river by simply passing along the escalating costs run up by a system they were instrumental in creating.

In effect, our health care system combines the best of capitalism with the worst of socialism in an explosive mixture that has sent health costs rising like a mushroom cloud. From a capitalistic perspective, providers are free to practice where they want, and in what specialty they want, and to charge what prices they want for services. Likewise, patients are free to go to whatever doctor they prefer to visit.

But, socialism creeps in when it is time to pay the bill. Providers dip into the ever-so-deep well of money called prepaid health insurance. Experts discussing this system call it the "third party payer system," but what they mean is insurance, whether through a private company or through Medicare, Medicaid, or Workman's Compensation. And there is no limit to the number of times providers can go to the well.

This is where the process begins to unravel. Like the restaurant owner who orders food for the customer, physicians control about 80 percent of all demand for health care in this country; thus physicians control 80 percent of our health care expenditures. Physicians tell us, the patients, what we need, when we need it, and how much we need. And we, as customers, do not question the doctor's recommendation — we are immune from all costs as a result of the third-party payer system.

Finally, aside from financing an education (the average physician is about $80,000 in debt upon graduation) doctors don't have to invest as much in capital equipment and inventory as other businesses. They do have to pay for a nurse, an insurance administrator, and their office, if they are in private practice, but they DON'T have to pay for major diagnostic equipment needed to produce income. This equipment is paid for by the local hospital. Why? Because hospitals depend on doctors to fill up the beds. If buying the latest medical technology will accomplish this, it's a good investment for the hospital. Ask any hospital administrator who the hospital's customers really are. If he or she answers anything other than the doctors, it's a good bet that this particular administrator is either unemployed or working for the government. As a physician once told me when discussing a particular business investment, "Please understand, we doctors aren't used to paying for anything needed for us to make money."

Roll it all together — the private and government money, the near-monopoly specializations, captive audiences and subsidized equipment, and it's plain to see that for providers of health care, our system is truly one of the most lucrative economic engines ever created.

But this is not the end of the story. Let's take a look at what happens to our restaurant if we consider how human nature will affect its operation over time. One thing is pretty obvious: As more and more restauranteurs learn the rules of the game, they will realize that they should be in the high-end of the market. Why run a coffee shop when you can serve haute cuisine and make four times as much money per order? It's human nature.

Another thing that necessarily occurs is that customers find themselves being taken more and more for granted. Suppose they want seafood but there's only one seafood restaurant in town? They'll have to patronize that one restaurant, no matter how long it takes to be seated. The restaurant owner, having a monopoly, will only pay middling attention to the customer's happiness.

23

And what about the insurance company which ostensibly pays the bill? Does it ever call the restaurant patrons to ask them about quality? How was the food? Did you really get all twelve courses that appeared on the bill? How was the service? Did someone pull your chair out when you were seated?

Finally, human nature tells us that some smart restaurant owners will eventually realize that they can make more money by organizing the menu à la carte — that is, billing separately for the meat, the vegetables, each bread stick, each grain of salt — rather than by the traditional practice of charging one price for an entire meal.

Today, the great majority of physicians are becoming subspecialists who command far higher incomes than the lowly general practitioner. And patients are spending more and more time in the waiting rooms and closet-sized examining rooms being examined, reexamined, and answering the same questions over and over for nurses, interns, and subspecialty residents (all of whom get paid for this redundant attention) before seeing the over-scheduled specialists.

And piece-meal billing — called "unbundling"— is rampant. (The needle goes in, the needle goes out. One stitch — but two separate à la carte charges.)

Human nature would foretell one further event in our restaurant saga. After all the trends to four-star French restaurants, à la carte billing, and so forth, and with costs going through the roof, eventually the employers (remember, the ones who are ultimately paying for all this) would balk at having to pay so much to keep their employees fed. Some employers would start their own restaurants, run by licensed professionals on their own payroll, because they could feed their employees for less than the restaurants from the "open" market. Some would demand that the insurance companies to which they have paid premiums for all these years would start looking out for their interests too.

Eventually, so many employers would start to demand a legitimate business relationship that insurance companies would become quite concerned. After years of coziness with the restaurant owners, the insurance companies would scramble to shift their allegiance to the employers, who are, after all, their customers.

The insurance companies would attempt to respond to their customers' complaints about skyrocketing costs. And they would question the restaurant owner's decisions. Does this customer really need that second slice of apple pie? Why didn't you serve them the domestic Cabernet instead of the vintage Bordeaux? Eventually, the restaurant business would be swamped with enormous red tape created by all these controls. And some restaurant owners would start playing cat-and-mouse games with the insurance companies, in efforts to elude the controls. This sad, muddled, budget-breaking state of affairs, all but paralyzed by red tape, is unfortunately the condition in which we find our health care system in 1994.

WHERE WE'RE HEADING...

If you think things are bad now, just wait until the turn of the century. In a report issued in December 1991, the Families USA Foundation spelled out, in horrifying detail, just how much we'll be paying for our profligate health care system if we don't rein costs in. Its findings: American families paid an average of $4,296 each in 1991 to support our health-care system. This figure included what families pay out of pocket for health care, for health-insurance premiums, for the Medicare payroll tax, for Medicare premiums, and general taxes to local, state and federal governments that are spent on health care. By 2000, the foundation estimated, this would rise to $9,397 — an astounding 429 percent more than the $1,742 the average family paid in 1980.

Average annual health payments by families amounted to 11.7 percent of family income in 1991, up from 9 percent in 1980, but this was projected to rise to 16.4 percent by 2000. Businesses' spending on health care, $237.6 billion in 1991, was projected to rise to $511.4 billion by 2000.

SO WHAT ARE THE FACTS?

a. Where does the U.S. rank internationally in the creation and production of medical technology?

b. What is the fastest job growth segment in the USA?

c. In 1992, what percent of the U.S. population was older than 65?

d. What percent of all health care resources does the U.S. population older than 65 utilize?

Answers:

a. First

b. Health care administration

c. 12%

d. 30%

CHAPTER 2:
GREAT LIES AND
SCAPEGOATS

When any opportunity as lucrative as our system for providing health care comes along, there are inevitable rationalizations, forwarded by those who have the most to benefit from the system, to explain and justify the seemingly unjustifiable sums of money involved.

For instance, the defense contractor who charges the government $600 for a wrench will stammer about how the price of the wrench really reflects administrative and development costs involved in completing the entire project. And the $250 coffee maker aboard the long-range patrol plane? Well, it has to be made to operate at high altitude and stand G-forces that no earth-bound coffee maker would ever experience. All this costs, you know.

So it is with our medical system. You can hear all sorts of reasons why our health costs are rising so disastrously. These justifications don't really address the crux of what ails our health care system. They are the Great Lies and Scapegoats of the current health care debate. Each of the factors mentioned does in fact contribute to our escalating health bill. But by focusing on them we fall for the classic misdirection play. We miss the core of the matter. With all that has been written and spoken about health care reform, we have heard these justifications repeated by "experts" of all kinds in all kinds of forums. Malpractice and defensive medicine, the aging population, the proliferation of technology, cost-shifting, the cost of drugs, and medical red tape. Let's put each of these in the proper perspective.

THE GREAT LIES

MALPRACTICE AND DEFENSIVE MEDICINE

The first great lie is that health costs are so high because doctors have to do more procedures than are really warranted, because if they don't they may be sued for malpractice. This justification fails to mention that health care providers are paid for all of these extra procedures they perform. And as we will see later, some feel obligated to perform many more extra procedures than others. Given the financial incentives involved, only the physician who orders the test may ever really know whether there is a genuine need for the additional procedure. It's very easy to justify, perhaps subliminally, on a variety of fronts, especially if you're a doctor with three kids in college.

More to the point, the AMA would have us believe that malpractice is a major factor in the cost of health care. "Tort reform" is a perennial favorite in every AMA position paper on how to control health costs. But let's look at just what the defensive costs are. Despite the official hand wringing, they are not in the insurance premiums doctors have to pay. Although to listen to them, physicians struggle to simply make ends meet after paying their malpractice insurance. Over the past ten years, malpractice insurance costs have actually declined and today average only about 4 percent of a physician's annual gross income. This level is not out of line with any other major insurance coverage, in other sectors of our economy, whether it is product liability for a manufacturer, or directors' and officers' liability for general corporate operations, or environmental liability insurance for chemical companies. And whatever the cost, malpractice premiums are built into virtually all of the fee schedules.

Consider a conversation I overheard at a golf practice range in 1988. Two doctors were standing within earshot. Doctor No. 1 said, "Congratulations. I understand you have now limited your OB/GYN practice to just GYN. I'll bet your malpractice costs went down considerably." To which Doctor No. 2 replied, "Thanks. But we never cared about malpractice costs. We just added the annual cost increase to our fees and passed it through."

"Just passed it through." How many business can simply "just pass it through" without customer resistance to rising costs? According to the American Medical Association, 1991 malpractice premiums paid by all the physicians in the United States totaled $5.18 billion. Unquestionably, that is a lot of money; but what is $5 billion out of total health spending that year of $850 billion? Not even one percent.

But wait, says the health lobby. The real cost of malpractice is all the extra things we have to do to avoid being sued. THAT'S the true cost of malpractice, and THAT'S why we need tort reform. Well, it's true that doctors do perform extra procedures to avoid being sued. It's a by-product of our litigation-happy society and modern medicine's own success. Americans have gotten spoiled by our medical prowess, and, as one obstetrician has said, most Americans now hold it as an article of faith that if there's not a perfect outcome and a perfect baby, somebody has to pay. Certainly the trial lawyers would like to make this the eleventh commandment. And doctors know there will always be a medical litigation specialist, with just enough knowledge to be dangerous, ready to use the gift of 20/20 hindsight to second-guess everything. Doctors are absolutely warranted in their complaints about the predatory practices of certain lawyers and their medical experts. (And with the continuous loosening of individual accountabilty by the courts we can expect continuing increases in the number of newly respectable predators.)

But are these extra tests really a major cause of soaring health costs? Not nearly. The fact is, no one really knows how many tests, scans, X-rays, physicals, shots, consultations, exploratory procedures and other medical services are delivered solely out of fear of being sued. In 1989, the AMA estimated this cost at $15 billion. But in February 1993 the National Medical Liability Reform Coalition released a study it commissioned from the health-research firm Lewin VHI that put the cost of defensive medicine at perhaps $6 billion to $7 billion a year. The difference, said Danny Mendelson, one of the study authors, was that Lewin weeded out all the procedures that, while they could be considered defensive, also had some marginal benefit to the patient. But even if you accept the AMA's figure, total it up — $5 billion in malpractice premiums and $15 billion in unnecessary procedures — and you get $20 billion. That's $20 billion out of $850 billion in 1992, which is still less than 5 percent of our health bill that year. Let's also not forget that of the $15 billion, at least $3 billion went directly into the pockets of the providers in the form of direct fees. That's a lot of money, so much that it is legitimate to wonder if all of the medical profession really wants tort reform. Maybe they just feel safe calling for it, knowing all the time that the trial lawyers will never let it happen.

THE AGING POPULATION

The second great lie is that health costs are going up because of our aging population. In 1992, 12 percent of the population was over 65. By 2040, it will be 20 percent. In raw terms, it is true that health costs mount as one ages, because the longer one lives the more time one will have to partake of the system, just as one has more opportunity to use lawyers and eat seafood. But it's not that simple. The problem, says the medical lobby, is that per capita spending for those over 65 is seven times that of someone in their teens — $745 vs. $5,340. The inference they wish you to draw is that because of that per-capita cost, we automatically are incurring higher health costs that we cannot avoid as we find ourselves with more elderly people to treat.

Let's look at another statistic that sheds a more realistic light on the matter. According to the Health Care Financing Administration (HCFA), a government agency that monitors medical spending, of all the money spent on medical care for a person, fully half of it will be spent in the last 60 days of life. Twenty-five percent of all Medicare expenditures for the elderly are spent for only one percent of the recipients, and this occurs during their last year of life.

Think of what happens in those last desperate days to save a life . . . the days spent in intensive or coronary care, the monitors affixed like strands of spaghetti, the emergency surgery, the against-all-hope transplants . . . It's easy to see how the money is spent.

Yet to be honest, much of this futile spending is demanded by the public. It's what the dean of one medical school calls the "Aunt Tilly syndrome." It goes like this: The doctor comes in and says "Aunt Tilly is gravely ill," and the family, freed by their insurance coverage of the financial consequences of their words, says, "Do everything you can to save her." Is the family wrong to do this? Not entirely. Through generations of TV medical shows we've come to expect miraculous cures and we've been conditioned to believe that there is no malady that technology cannot overcome. So we say, "Do everything you can." And if it was our aunt in the other room, who wouldn't say the same?

It's understandable.

But we must also understand that the system may not really want to do anything about this. Remember, all that last-ditch spending is somebody's income. It's telling that the American Medical Association, which has been dragged kicking and screaming into the debate over reforming health care, now is pushing for a health plan whose basic benefits would not include paying for hospice care. Hospice services allow people to go home to die. In peace. With compassion. Without all the chest-pounding and last-minute surgeries that people who die in hospitals must endure. Hospice services also are cheap, compared to hospitals. But think: Hospice care doesn't contribute to physicians' incomes. So why should providers want a medical plan to cover something like that?

But even when families realize that spending is useless, medical practitioners have become so accustomed to extraordinary measures that often they just won't take no for an answer.

I found this out the hard way after my mother-in-law died. She was terminally ill with cancer and less than a week from death. The medical staff at the hospital was recommending a new round of chemotherapy treatment even though they acknowledged that she was terminal. There was no hope of recovery, yet if our family had allowed the chemotherapy to occur the cost would have been many more thousands of dollars, which the insurance company would have paid. Furthermore, there was real probability that the treatment might actually hasten her death. At best it would simply have protracted an emotionally and physically painful state.

Within days she died, making the issue moot. But later, when the medical bills arrived there was an unremembered charge of $400 for a surgical consultation several days before her death. What was especially perplexing is that no surgery was performed, and in fact, none was ever contemplated by our family. Upon inquiry, it was discovered that this surgeon claimed he was asked to review the medical chart "in case surgery might be necessary." Surgery? Three days before death, when we had already refused a final offer of chemotherapy! Try as I might, I never determined who allegedly ordered the consultation. In fact, it appeared to be a distinct possibility that this surgeon simply read all the charts at the nurses station and forwarded consultation charges as a matter of routine. Obviously, we never paid the bill, nor did the surgeon or his collection agent even pursue the matter. If someone legitimately owed you $400, wouldn't you try to collect it?

Absent the Aunt Tilly syndrome, and a family's request for heroic efforts to save a dying person's life, the scenario for health spending for the elderly becomes more like that for the population in general. And who is prescribing this medical care? Right. The doctors.

Consider the revolution in treating cardiovascular disease precipitated by a procedure called cardiac catherization — a treatment for heart disease that is reasonably inexpensive and much less risky than bypass surgery. For instance, an angioplast or an ultrasound can be performed on an outpatient surgery basis for $3,000 to $6,000, compared with $60,000 to $100,000 for a bypass.

A year ago, while I was having a tour of the cardiac catherization clinic at a major medical center in the Southeast, the clinical director proudly showed me the bar charts showing that the number of these bypass alternatives done at his facility had increased from 17 ten years ago to 3,500 today — more than one percent of all such procedures performed annually in the United States. Upon hearing this, I remarked to the beaming physician that his colleagues, the chest cutters (bypass specialists), must be upset that the mounting rate of these alternative procedures was threatening to put them out of business. The doctor's face suddenly turned bright red. "No," he said sheepishly. "It should be that way," he said, "but in fact the number of bypass operations is going up, too, just not as quickly as the alternative procedures."

It took another doctor some weeks later to explain this seeming incongruity to me. She said, quite candidly, that the cheaper alternatives had not eliminated the expensive bypasses; bypasses have simply shifted their demographics. They are now done on a much older population, only after all the 50, 60, and 70-year-olds have had multiple doses of the cheap stuff. She then told me of an 82-year-old patient who recently had a bypass. In her opinion, a first angioplast would have been sufficient, but for what ever reason this patient had been convinced by the surgeon that the bypass was the appropriate treatment. After a heated debate between physicians, the bypass was performed. Her conclusion, voiced privately, was the same as mine: By all rights the number of bypasses should be declining, not increasing.

What has happened? We've simply added another course to the menu, prescribed by the restaurant owner who ordered our dinner. The cheaper procedures have been relegated to the status of appetizers and major surgery has become the main course.

ALL TECHNOLOGY INCREASES COSTS

The third and the biggest of the great lies, and one that we hear the most about these days, is the mixed blessing we've received from advances in medical technology. Modern medical technology saves lives, no doubt about it, but because of it, costs have gone up. Unwarily, the public has bought this load of propaganda that allegedly justifies the massive increase in health care costs. Yes, modern medical technology — the PET scanners, the CAT scanners, the lithotripters, the lasers, the miniature scalpels and cameras that are snaked into the body everywhere — has contributed substantially to our mounting health costs.

But, this is only because these medical wonders are being wielded in a system that allows those doing the wielding to pass on every conceivable cost to those paying the bill. In a true free market economy, as we have in virtually all other aspects of our society, new technology reduces costs — just look at what has happened to computer prices and the effect of computers on workplace efficiency.

What should occur when new technology enters the market place? Suppose a building contractor invests in a new type of pneumatic nailer that reduces the time workers usually spend driving nails in a house. Because this new tool makes the crew more efficient, the house can be framed in one-third the time, bringing a considerable cost savings to the contractor. Because the crew is now so efficient, the contractor can become more competitive by submitting lower bids, and more houses can be built in the same amount of time. Essentially, it's the same strategy used at Walmart or UPS — make the system so efficient that although you make less profit per unit, you make considerably more money because of your increased volume.

Now let's see at what happens in health care. Let's consider for example the widespread use of lithotripters — the machines that pulverize kidney stones with sound waves. Before the lithotripter came along in the mid-1980s, the only way to get rid of a kidney stone was to pass it, or to submit to being sliced open, itself a lengthy operation that involved a painful and slow recovery. But with the lithotripter, you can walk into a day surgery center, be tripped, and walk out again within a few hours. Now, you figure, what should cost more: a stay in the hospital, complete with invasive surgery, anesthesiology, recovery room charges, and all, or a few hours having a lithotripter with ultrasound. Well of course, the surgery costs more. But not by much.

The 1992 annual report by Blue Cross and Blue Shield of North Carolina noted that the average charge for surgical treatment of kidney stones was $7,773. The average charge for lithotripsy was $7,438 — only $335 less.

Technology such as the lithotripter has made providers extremely more efficient. Like the contractor, Walmart or UPS, they too can handle much more volume at much less risk of malpractice. But unlike the real world of the free market, two things have happened to subvert the normal impact that increased efficiency has on prices: First, many doctors see it as a matter of right that their incomes should go up (say 10 percent) every year, at least to keep up with inflation if nothing else. Isn't everybody entitled to a pay raise once a year? But even as they raise fees, their unit costs are decreasing because new technology is allowing them to complete many more units in much less time. And secondly, doctors are right when they say that technology costs money, and they simply pass the cost of this technology on to the patient as an additional part of their escalating fee structure. An MRI scanner costs at least $2 million. Devices that cost $2 million or $3 million abound, and time and again physicians and hospitals have recovered the cost of this equipment within a matter of months.

A normal business rule of thumb, which is also built into the Internal Revenue Code, is that it takes three to seven years to recover the cost of capital equipment, not three to seven months! It is common to see doctors making in excess of 100 percent annual returns on one such investment. When the average charge for an MRI scan in the United States is about $1,000, compared with $177 in Japan, it is easy to see why. It is also easy to see why there are more MRI scanners in Duke University Hospital than in all of the city of Toronto.

One of the best examples of the real cost of new technology to our health system is the field of ophthalmic surgery. A few years ago it took several hours to remove a cataract from the eye. Today with the use of advanced technology, a cataract can be removed in 8 minutes at much less risk to the patient, or to the surgeon for malpractice. In a normal competitive market, surgeon's fees should go down (just like they do in law or accounting when word processors make the professional more efficient), but in fact they have gone up.

Our hospitals and clinics now have cataract "factories" where surgeons remove as many as 50 cataracts a day. The surgeon's fee, not including the additional charges for equipment and the operating room, can run as high as $3,000 per cataract.

Working at full capacity, a surgeon could pull in a cool $150,000 in a day. Not a bad income! It is about 10 times the national average annual income of $14,500 in 1992 and 17 times the annual wages of a worker employed forty hours a week for minimum wage.

But WAIT! We are not talking about a YEAR we are talking about ONE DAY! If the cataract surgeon performs 50 operations in a day, the pay is 3,000 times that of the average America wage earner. And 6,000 times the earnings of the millions of hospital employees across the country who work for the minimum wage. Even a surgeon who performs only a tenth of that number would earn a wage hundreds of times that of most of the rest of America's workers.

But why should this be a problem? If the market will bear it, what business is it of ours how much the professional can charge or how many procedures can be done in a day?

It's a problem because all the specialists performing more procedures per day, and charging more per procedure, has an enormous net impact on our total national health bill. Remember, it's the total health bill that is causing insurance rates to rise, pricing more people out of the market, which in turn leads to cost shifting to those who are left to pay the ever higher premiums. (And tangentially these enormous earnings affect all the rest of us by their inflationary impact on the cost of housing, goods, and services in our communities.)

But there's another principle involved here, too. It's not that these providers are getting the market rate. There IS no market rate. They're setting it themselves, then invoicing an insurance company that will pay the fee as long as it is "usual and customary." The insurance companies, and historically Medicare and Medicaid, have allowed providers to set their own charges. Unfortunately however, the way that "usual and customary" charges are determined flies in the face of every anticompetitive law in the land. Do we really believe doctors don't know what the office up the street is charging? Yet, typically insurance companies say the determination of "usual and customary" is 90 percent of the highest "biller" in town.

Why 90 percent? Because the insurance company says so, and because they have historically been able to simply pass increases through to the corporate employer while taking their administrative cut. (Don't forget, 1.74 percent of a billion dollars is more than 1.74 percent of a million dollars — even for a "not for profit" corporate administrator.)

THE SCAPEGOATS

COST SHIFTING

"Cost shifting" is the health industry's term for what happens when the cost of caring for the indigent is moved to the paying customer.

It's a consequence of having 37 million people without health insurance. These people don't go without medical care. They show up at hospital emergency rooms, usually after their problem has reached a stage where it will cost much more to treat than if it had been nipped in the bud.

But the terrible truth is, that even though we do not insure the health of 13 percent of our population, so far that has been only a minor part of the cost-shift. The biggest offender behind cost-shifting is the federal government. Every time a patient on Medicaid (poor people) or Medicare (elderly people) sees the doctor or goes to the hospital — patients whose medical care is supposedly paid for by the government — the government skips out on a major part of the bill.

For Medicaid patients who go to the hospital, the government pays a fixed amount for every day that the patient is admitted. Whether the patient is there for open-heart surgery or a hangnail, the payment for the room, meals, etc., is the same. Inevitably, this means that hospitals lose money on these patients. They make it up by charging the loss to other patients who pay out of their pocket or who have insurance. This daily payment, coincidentally, is not based on any rational standard such as the cost of living or average medical costs. In fact, the payment can vary by literally hundreds of dollars per day for hospitals in the same city. Why? Because back when Medicaid was installed in 1965, it established an individual benchmark for every hospital in the United States, based on that hospital's operating costs at the time the system was implemented. Typically, the large, sophisticated medical centers and teaching hospitals had significantly higher costs than the community hospitals. So their per diem rate was initially set much higher, and has stayed considerably higher through subsequent adjustments for inflation. In effect, as the financial administrator of one efficient hospital lamented, the hospitals that were the most efficient have been penalized the most ever since.

Because of the sheer number of patients involved, Medicare has been an even bigger factor in cost shifting. With Medicare patients, the government retained its principle of making fixed payments, but it based the payment not per day (like Medicaid), but per disease. Through an incredible exercise in bureaucracy, the Medicare system has pigeon-holed every conceivable disease into what it calls Diagnostic Related Groups, or the famous (or infamous) DRGs.

When Medicare first initiated DRGs, the theory was sound: Give the hospitals a fixed payment and give them incentive to control costs by letting them keep any surplus. But in practice it's been a disaster, for two reasons. First, the annual increases in DRG reimbursements have not kept up with the torrid pace of medical inflation. So even efficient hospitals, which initially could make a profit from Medicare patients, soon found Medicare becoming a fiscal sink hole. The second reason is that several years after implementation, the bureaucrats changed the ground rules and declared that henceforth, Medicare would pay either the standard DRG payment or the actual cost of treating the patient, whichever was less. The net effect was to wipe out any incentive to control costs. The DRG payment meant to be a ceiling became the floor instead. Immediately, no Medicare patient was ever treated for less than the DRG cost. Maybe the difference was only $15, but multiply $15 by the 34 million Medicare recipients and we've added more than $500 million to our national health bill.

So, you ask, how does his affect you? It affects you plenty. Remember, the hospitals are shifting losses to their paying patients, and this puts fees on a vicious upward cycle. Let's say it costs a hospital $150 to put a patient up for a night in a semi-private room. If everyone paid the bill, that's what everyone would be charged per night for the room — $150. But everybody (including the federal government, as we have seen) does not pay. So the hospital charges everyone $200 a night. But this just makes the hospital lose all the more money — instead of being out $150 from the non-paying patient, it's out $200. So it has to raise rates a little more to make up for this greater loss — and this in turn creates yet another shortfall. The system is programmed for ever-increasing costs at almost every point.

But there's an even greater catch: You're paying for all these costs that are shifted even if you never spend a day in the hospital or receive any out-patient services. Why? The answer lies in how health insurance works in general. Insurance companies assign policy holders (even corporate policies with many employees) to risk pools that comprise a given population. The criteria for a population may be age, occupation, or past health history, but whatever it is, you are put in a pool. The insurance premiums are based on the cost of providing health care for the year for everyone in that pool. If anyone in the pool goes to the hospital or receives medical treatment (which is a virtual certainty) then their bill will include the costs shifted to it from Medicare and Medicaid patients. And since premiums for the pool are based, in part, on the necessity to absorb the underpayment in Medicaid and Medicare, the overall costs for the insurance pool are higher than if the pool stood alone.

Mind you, this is not some academic exercise. There are huge sums of money involved. For every hospital dollar billed in 1992 to a privately paying patient or insurance company, 32 cents was the cost of treating someone else, either a Medicare or Medicaid patient, or someone without any health insurance at all. If current trends continue unabated, by 1996 the cost-shift will be fully 50 percent of every hospital bill.

This has led to the irrational situation, pointed out by the chairman of family medicine at a prominent medical school, that the medical care of affluent retirees entitled to Medicare is being subsidized by younger workers who may be much worse off financially.

More significantly, there is an even more costly result of the cost-shifting that has trapped our medical system in a vicious spiral. As medical bills go up because of cost-shifting, insurance companies have had to raise their premiums. This leads more people to drop their health insurance because they can't afford the higher premium, which means they become part of the medically indigent whose care has to be cost-shifted to the remaining people who can pay. It's like many cities in the United States—they have raised taxes so high they have effectively run off a large percentage of the corporate tax base, leaving fewer and fewer corporate employers to pay for the growing government bureaucracies.

DRUGS COST TOO MUCH

Drug companies are convenient whipping boys when it comes to assigning blame for our soaring medical bills. And they're an easy mark. They hawk new medications that can cost up to hundreds of dollars a dose. To be sure, drug companies have exploited the same weakness in our health-care system that is the root cause for all its ailments: All too often the person taking the drug was not the person who paid the drug company for the prescription. So why do I call drug prices a scapegoat? Because of two important differences that distinguish drug companies from most other aspects of our health-care system.

First, and foremost, is the simple fact that there IS competition in the drug market. Over the past decade the use of so-called "generic drugs," which cost far less than brand-names, has exploded. Today generics can be found for everything from night-time cold medications to ulcer medications such as Tagamet, to heart medications such as Lanoxin and Cardizem. The rise of generics has corresponded with the struggle to control medical costs. Insurance companies and HMO's, armed with clinical studies showing generics to be as effective as the brand-names, have increasingly required their patients to use generics. The competition in the drug marketplace is very far from perfect. Drug companies, upon introducing a new medication, get exclusive rights to the formula for a set period of time before other companies can market generic versions. Given the huge amounts of money drug companies spend on research and development ($10.9 billion in 1992 alone), and the lengthy process and clinical trials the FDA requires before it can go out to the pharmacies in America, it is only fair to give them a franchise on new drugs.

The second reason I call drug prices a scapegoat is that even through drug companies take their money from the money well called insurance, they can't go to the well without the cooperation of doctors. Unless a doctor prescribes a certain medication, the patient simply can't get it. Hence all the advertising aimed at promoting patient visits to doctors. Hair loss? see your doctor. Too fat? see your doctor. Please, doctor, just keep signing those prescription pads.

THE MEDICAL BUREAUCRACY

The administrative burden in medicine has reached cosmic proportions. The *Future Shock* predictions of bureaucracy run amok, with bureaucrats to check on the bureaucrats who check on the bureaucrats, has come true. We are already in the future in health care.

Consider the case of Forsyth Memorial Hospital, an 800-bed regional medical center in North Carolina: This hospital has three people who work full time pre-certifying patients for admission, three people who translate patient charts into the codes needed to submit claims, seven people who review patient charts to make sure that patients still need to be in the hospital (lest the insurance company refuse payment), three people who double check on the seven to make sure that patients do not receive unreimbursable tests, and two who do nothing but answer letters from insurance and federal administrators who are challenging what the hospital does.

Surely, you say, this much bureaucracy must be unusual. Not so. Forsyth is one of the best run hospitals in the country. Its ratio of patients to employees is 1 to 3.8, which is near the bottom of a scale that ranges nationally from about 1 to 3 to 1 to 8. A state ranking gave it the lowest costs of the state's 17 largest hospitals.

All this, of course, is what one hospital goes through just to keep the insurance companies happy and keep the cash flowing. Why is all this necessary? Much has to do with the sheer complexity of insurance. In the United States, more than 1,500 different companies sell health insurance. And unfortunately, each one of them has its own way of doing things. Its own forms, its own rules for which procedures have to be pre-approved, its own levels of deductibles for various categories of treatment and so on and so on. Even within the same insurance company, the ground rules may vary wildly from patient to patient.

Let's say Sara and Jane work for two different employers which provide health insurance to their employees through a fictitious insurance company that I will call Good Health. Sara's company is doing well and has bought an extensive policy from Good Health. So Sara gets an annual physical for free and she pays only half the cost of annual physicals for her children. Jane's company has taken a beating and has been reducing benefits, so the policy Jane's company bought doesn't cover annual physicals. Sara's policy includes mammograms and pap smears. Jane's doesn't. For catastrophic care, Sara has a $250 annual deductible and then the policy pays 100 percent. Jane's deductible is $500 and then the policy pays 80 percent, up to a total out of pocket cost of $2,000.

This is a simple example, but you get the point. In practice, the hair-splitting from the employees of one company to those of another can be far more extensive as insurance companies have tailored policies to accommodate each customer. Theoretically, it's the patient's responsibility to deal with his or her insurance company. But, it doesn't work that way in practice. Virtually every doctor's office and hospital submits insurance claims for its patients and collects the payment directly, because that is its best chance for receiving payment.

But this means that every hospital, every walk-in emergency clinic, every doctor in private practice has to hire people who can master a maze of rules, deductibles and claim forms. Woe to those who do not. All it takes is one misplaced comma or one block of missing information and the insurance company will deny payment.

Virtually any doctor can tell numerous stories of claims for minor amounts that were kicked back several times over. It's not unknown for a particular claim to be bounced back and forth for two years, to a point where the combined cost in manpower spent on the collection far exceeds the amount of the claim. As one physician explained, "They're just looking for any little reason to deny you payment."

Why are the insurance companies so picky? Because the longer they can forestall paying, the longer they can keep the premium money and earn interest on it. With medical costs rising so fast, insurance companies have to do everything they can to stay profitable. And being picky makes them money.

Given all this red tape, is it any surprise that the percentage of people employed in health care has grown from 3 percent of all private, nonagricultural workers in the U.S. in 1980 to 9 percent in 1991? The upshot of all this hiring is the absurd situation in which Blue Cross/Blue Shield of Massachusetts has more people on the payroll to administer claims for just that one state than the Canadian health system uses for its whole country.

This fact has been cited by Public Citizen Health Care Group, the Ralph Nader organization that is pushing for a "single-payer system" similar to Canada's, where all medical clams are sent to a single agency responsible for administering the health care for everyone in the country. There is one set of rules for everybody, there are no legions of administrators, and none of the Mickey Mouse games over claims that are so common in our country. In fact, Public Citizen says that if our health system were administered as efficiently as Canada's, we would have saved $193 billion in 1992. That's certainly an exaggeration. As Christopher Conover, a health care expert at Duke University points out, some of our administrative costs — particularly the cost of pre-certification before performing certain procedures or admitting people to the hospital — do actually help retard medical spending.

The fact is, no one really knows how much cost red tape has added to our health bill, but common sense tells us that it's considerable. The General Accounting Office estimated the cost of excess bureaucracy at $67 billion. *Consumer Reports* put the cost of red tape and fraud at $200 billion.

So why is the enormous excess bureaucracy a straw man? Because virtually all of this bureaucracy has been created in response to the runaway costs of health care, costs that were created by a system without incentives to be both high quality and cost effective. As insurance companies and the government began to face up to losses they began clamping down on the doctors and patients in an attempt to control costs. They started making doctors call before putting a patient in the hospital. To discourage frivolous visits to the doctor, they began requiring that patients pay deductibles. Initially, the deductibles were nominal amounts, but now deductibles of $1,000 a year or more are common. For people enrolled in health maintenance organizations, copayments have been instituted in the hope of having much the same effect. If you have to pay $10 for every visit to the HMO, you won't go there as often, or so the reasoning goes.

All this would seem to validate the conclusion of the president of the American Hospital Association. "The only way to reduce health costs is to provide less health care." This is exactly what insurance companies, through copayments, deductibles and pre-admission requirements, are trying to do: Reduce health spending by discouraging the delivery of health care.

But as we shall see, this approach is like trying to sink a finishing nail with a sledge hammer. Undoubtedly, we need to reduce the delivery of some health care, but it's only certain types of health care that must be addressed, not all health care. And care must be delivered through a system in which those who create the demand, the providers, are motivated to do so at the highest qualitative level but at the lowest possible cost.

A LITTLE BEDSIDE MANNER
GOES A LONG WAY

Physicians who show effective, empathetic bedside manners get sued less than those who don't, even when things don't work out the way they should.

In 1991 the AMA surveyed public opinion about doctors and found that 58 percent did not think their doctor explained things to them adequately, 63 percent believe that doctors are too interested in money, and 69 percent said they were losing faith in doctors.

A Harris Poll of people who switched doctors found that 51 percent did not think their old doctor spent enough time with them and 42 percent said their doctor was not friendly.

*Other studies flesh out these findings: **General practitioners spend an average of only 7 minutes with a patient per visit and as a rule they interrupt within 18 seconds of the patient's explanation of the ailment.** One upshot of all this is that 80 percent of physicians never hear all their patients' complaints.*

The situation has reached the point that medical schools at the University of California and the University of Illinois have pilot programs using mock patients to evaluate a student's bedside manner as a requirement for graduation. Whether the exercise will make any lasting difference on the practitioner is questionable. As one student put it, "Anyone can put on a show for 15 minutes."

SO WHAT ARE THE FACTS?

a. In 1981, how many cardiac angioplasty procedures were performed in the U.S.?

b. In 1981, how many heart bypasses were performed?

c. In 1990, how many cardiac angioplasty procedures were performed?

d. In 1990, how many heart bypasses were performed?

e. In 1962 what percent of all doctors were in
primary care fields?

f. In 1993, what percent of all doctors were
subspecialists?

Answers:

a. 6,000

b. 159,000

c. 285,000

d. 392,000

e. 85%

f. 85% — a complete reversal since 1962.

CHAPTER 3:
ALL PHYSICIANS ARE NOT CREATED EQUAL: IS THERE A GENERAL PRACTITIONER IN THE HOUSE?

When it comes to medicine, Americans want the best. Our medical community has responded: With more new devices, with cutting-edge medical technology and most of all, with the development of an extensive network of subspecialists who make their living treating only certain ailments. If you have a foot problem, you can go to a podiatrist. A mysterious and itchy skin rash? That calls for a dermatologist. Chronic abdominal gas? Better see a gastroenterologist. No part of our anatomy is without its specialists. No ailment is without its "expert" practitioner. For whatever ails us, there is a community of specially trained doctors who make it their business (yes, their business) to deal with it.

So what's wrong with that? Aren't we entitled to the better care a specialist will give since he knows so much more about the part of us that is ailing? Shouldn't this be more efficient? Well, there's nothing wrong with availing yourself of the best care you can get. But as we shall see, we pay dearly, individually and as a society, for this expertise.

The rise in subspecialization has been addressed all too often in medical journals. Inevitably, these articles piously lament the lack of primary care physicians — the general practitioners, the psysiatrists, the emergency room physicians, the family practitioners and the pediatricians — who historically formed the backbone of the medical community but who now are practically saints in today's medical environment. The decline of primary care physicians has hit rural areas the hardest. Most subspecialists gravitate to the cities with pools of patients big enough to sustain their practices, leaving fewer and fewer country doctors.

The medical community is well aware of what's been happening in its ranks. After some analysis, the AMA has come up with the reasons that medical students want to be specialists.

MEDICAL SCHOOL COSTS TOO MUCH

Medical students, one medical school department chairman has said, are so paralyzed with fear at the debt they incur to get through medical school that they feel forced into a subspecialty, which generally pays better than primary care fields. Perhaps some students are so paralyzed. But that does not explain why the vast majority of students who are already worried about their debts would then spend several additional years training as a subspecialist when they could go out and work for a very handsome living. (The answer is quite clear; at subspecialist compensation levels, the school debts are repaid rather quickly.)

THE MEDICAL SCHOOL ENVIRONMENT

Most medical students are trained these days in tertiary care centers — the major medical centers equipped to handled the most difficult cases and where doctors push the envelope of medical technology. All this has a great influence on impressionable young medical students, it is argued. Wowed by all the wonderful things that can be done in medicine these days, students decide they want to be part of the action. Why spend a career in family practice conducting school physicals when you can be unlocking the secrets of the brain, or pioneering new surgical techniques to repair clogged arteries?

PRESTIGE

This is a secondary effect of having medical schools in tertiary care centers. There's a pecking order in these temples of modern medical technology, and the primary care departments are at the bottom — if the school even offers a primary care curriculum at all.

Also, as the department head at one medical school explained, in academic medicine the research dollars, the lab space, the choicest offices all flow to the subspecialties. Research brings prestige, and that alone influences medical students who see the primary care doctors being treated like second-class citizens.

If you ask physicians about the flight to the subspecialties, they will usually get around to mentioning the higher salaries that subspecialists command. Usually, it's couched in terms of "another factor" or "a cynical interpretation" of why there are so few doctors going into primary care. But is it?

Let's return to our restaurant business. You have completed all of your schooling at the age of 28 or 29, and now it's time to decide what kind of restaurant you are going to open. You could run a hot dog stand. There's little up-front cost and if you pick the right corner you can be making good money from day one. Or, you can delay your career for another two or three years and learn the fine art of French cuisine. There are some other facts you are mulling over in trying to make a decision. If you run a hot dog stand, you will make an average of $3.50 per customer. That's not much, but again, if you put in a full day on the right street corner you'll have plenty of business and do just fine.

On the other hand, if you learn the art of French cooking and run the French restaurant, you'll make an average of $65 a customer — maybe twice that with appetizers, desert and a second bottle of wine. Also, you'll only have to work part of the day. And remember, in this restaurant business you do the ordering for your customers.

So if you're training to be a restauranteur, what are you going to do? You're going to open the French restaurant, of course. That's why virtually all of our doctors are going into subspecialties. It's the rational thing to do, given the way our medical system works. Since you control the demand, you can make the income you want; you are assured of payment because you send the bill to the insurance company. Why not go into a field where you can make hundreds of thousands of dollars more each year?

What's the alternative? To enter a family practice and spend the day switching gears from poison ivy, to stitching lacerations, to responding to the panicked calls from patients who think they might be having a heart attack? You spend your whole life rushing from one medical brush fire to the next, and then spend every night wondering if your beeper will go off. (Radiologists and thoracic surgeons don't get awakened at night.) Who would be willing to work longer hours for less pay when they can make more money and have nights and weekends free? Most of us would do the same thing that most doctors are doing — it's human nature.

How lucrative is it to be a subspecialist? It can be very lucrative. For instance, you can make more money in an hour as a surgeon than in a day as a general practitioner. And remember, even as a surgeon, YOU control the demand for your servvices.

General practitioners will always, tactfully, acknowledge that there are substantial differences in what they make and what subspecialists make. Numbers published by the AMA (which tend to be low) suggest that the specialists make a little more than twice as much. In 1990, for example, an AMA survey found that the average doctor in primary care made $102,700 in net income. The average surgeon made $236,400 that year. But don't for a minute believe these numbers.

The AMA's numbers are misleading because these "average" salaries include the greatly reduced (relatively speaking) earnings of every resident and fellow — people who technically are MD's but who are not yet in practice. The averages also are misleading because there is tremendous variation within the ranks.

For example, a survey by *Medical Economics* alleges that in 1989 cardiovascular surgeons made an average of $296,300 in net income — cash in hand, after office expenses, malpractice insurance, automobile allowances, continuing education, and pension plans. Thoracic surgeons, on the other hand, allegedly made a net income of $188,750.

The AMA report and the *Medical Economics* report are based on the honor system: Physicians telling the world what they earn. Private sources like banks, mortgage companies, and leasing companies with access to tax returns and financial statements show a different set of figures.

For doctors in practice for at least five years, the average net income (after office expenses, malpractice insurance, and so on) for general practitioners was more like $200,000 to $300,000. Radiologists and gastroenterologists averaged a take-home of \$350,000 to \$450,000, while the take-home income of neurosurgeons, cardiologists and orthopedic surgeons averaged in the range of \$600,000 to \$900,000. It is no longer surprising to find net incomes in the \$1 million plus range among subspecialists. Quite a vast difference from what the AMA or *Medical Economics* would have us believe.

You may never needlessly see a specialist, you may never go to the doctor in a given year, but your insurance premiums are still going to include the cost of all those people in your insurance pool who did. Since physicians' fees are about 25 percent of the nation's health bill, they are a major component of the costs that determines your health insurance premium. You can do the arithmetic yourself: Of the 650,000 doctors, if 85 percent are primary care physicians making \$100,000 a year and 15 percent are subspecialists making \$500,000 a year, the total fees received by these physicians is approximately \$100 billion. Now let's reverse the percentages, as is reality over the past 30 years. If the 15 percent primary care doctors make \$100,000 a year and the 85 percent subspecialists make \$500,000 a year, what's the total bill?

It's about \$286 billion. That's \$186 billion more that is going to be passed on by the insurance companies to the public. And we all pay dearly.

IS THERE A GENERAL PRACTITIONER
IN THE HOUSE?

(As reported in the New York Times*)*

Dr. Franklin Yee probably never thought that he would die because there are too many specialists on the loose. But Yee, a surgeon in Sacramento, did almost die after he developed a high fever, nausea and abdominal pains.

Thinking he might have an ulcer, Yee visited a trusted colleague who was a gastroenterologist. The gastroenterologist thought Yee might have some sort of heart virus, so he referred Yee to a cardiologist who ordered an electrocardiogram in case Yee had suffered a heart attack. The test looked normal but some of the readings looked suspicious, so the cardiologist put Yee into the coronary care unit. While in the unit, the pain shifted to Yee lower right abdomen, and Yee concluded that he had appendicitis. His son, also a doctor, confirmed his diagnosis. But the gastroenterologist demurred. Yee's bowels were active, so it couldn't be his appendix. He sent Yee home, but the next day the pain was worse than ever and his abdomen was bloated.

The cardiologist checked back and pronounced Yee's heart just fine. Now the specialists decided that Yee might be passing a kidney stone and took X-rays. They were normal. So they ordered a CT scan to attempt to unravel this mystery. The CT scan showed signs of a serious illness in which impaired blood flow can destroy the bowels. The cardiologist wanted to do an angiogram, and he also called in a vascular surgeon.

But Yee put his foot down. He insisted that they operate to remove his appendix, and the doctors humored him. But they didn't accept Yee's diagnosis. They felt they would have to remove a large area of damaged bowel and they ordered up large amounts of blood for transfusions. By now, almost three days had passed since Yee had consulted the gastroenterologist. When Yee woke up after the operation, the doctors told Yee that he had been right all along. But his appendix had ruptured and deadly bacteria had spread throughout his abdomen. After eight days of receiving antibiotics and being in constant pain, Yee finally went home, where he spent another four weeks convalescing.

The hospital bill, not counting doctors' fees, was $30,000, or about $20,000 more than if he had been operated on when he first went to the hospital. Insurance paid the bill.

SO WHAT ARE THE FACTS?

a. What percent of the low-back surgery performed is generally unnecessary?
b. What percent of tonsillectomies, hysterectomies and prostectomies are generally unnecessary?
c. What percent of health care expenditures are attributed to "quality waste" (i.e., to fix what should have been done right the first time)?

Answers:
a. 50%
b. 30%
c. 35%

CHAPTER 4:
NOT ALL BYPASSES ARE
GRAFTED EQUALLY

During a recent meeting of insurance executives, a prominent physician gave a presentation on something called "medical outcomes." It's the new catchword in the medical journals these days. "What is the outcome of this course of treatment?" "Did the surgery have a good outcome?" It's a great word for medicine — because it is just as subjective as the whole medical system. To doctors, outcome can mean just about anything they want it to mean.

Let's illustrate with an example we all can relate to: When Bo Jackson injured his hip playing football, he ended up having a total hip replacement. How is one to judge the outcome of his surgery? Does he have a successful outcome only if he plays football again? Or will it be successful if he can resume his baseball career, but not his football career? What if he can walk without pain for the rest of his life but he never plays football or baseball again? What if he simply didn't die during surgery? Is that a successful outcome? To his doctor, probably so. To Bo, probably not. "Outcomes," like beauty, are in the eye of the beholder.

Of course, with our society rightfully focusing on quality and cost effectiveness, it should be expected that medicine would be forced onto the bandwagon. But in spite of all the talk at seminars, and for all the ink and paper consumed in journals about outcomes, the truth of the matter is that there is almost no way to judge medical outcomes. As the head of one state's Blue Cross/Blue Shield admitted after a presentation on outcomes, insurance companies have very little means for making quality distinctions between and among providers. It's subjective on their part too.

Why are outcomes in the eye of the beholder? Because we have no yardsticks by which to measure a provider's performance. The fact is, less than 33 percent of all medical procedures have any database on outcomes to help the doctor or the medical consumer evaluate effectiveness of treatment. Of that 33 percent, only about half are based on any scientific evaluation with "double blind" studies. Thus only about 16 percent of all medical procedures have any arm's-length scientific data to support their use. Virtually all of that 16 percent consists of drug trials, conducted at the behest of the Food and Drug Administration.

In effect most of the medical procedures (as opposed to medications) performed in this country have never been evaluated scientifically for their effectiveness. It is not unlike an expensive and risky game of blind man's bluff.

What happens in a medical system where there are no quality distinctions? Let's stop and consider two scenarios, drawn from real life, involving real physicians. The first scenario is set in the home of an orthopedic surgeon. A friend has dropped by for an impromptu visit. The surgeon's wife tells the friend that her husband is in the basement. The friend walks down the stairs, and is quite shocked by the scene. There on the table is the amputated leg from a cadaver. The surgeon is working on the leg and barely looks up. Seeing the shocked look on his friend's face, he feels compelled to explain: "I've got a knee replacement scheduled for the morning and I've never done one. I thought I'd better practice."

The second scenario involves an orthopedic back specialist who spent four years of residency at one of the nation's premier teaching hospitals: Massachusetts General, one of the hospitals where Harvard trains doctors. In all four years of his residency, this back specialist, a doctor trained to make his living diagnosing and treating maladies of the back, has not once set foot in the hospital's physical therapy department. Never mind that 88 percent of all back injuries are muscular in nature and require physical therapy. This doctor was too busy learning all the latest surgical techniques for operating on backs to even observe the therapy required in the overwhelming majority of cases.

What's the result of training back specialists without teaching them about the physical side of treating lower back pain? It can be summarized in two statistics: (1) According to most medical estimates, 50 percent of all back surgery in the United

States is unnecessary, and (2) In the United States, doctors perform seven times more back surgery, per capita, than in the country with the second highest rate of back surgery, which is the United Kingdom.

What's the lesson to be drawn? It is this: If 50 percent of back surgery in this country is not necessary and we do seven times more back surgery here than in any other country in the world, the conclusion, as our Harvard trained back specialist shows, is that doctors are cutting people open because that's what doctors are trained to do. And if the wound from the surgery heals, they can tell themselves that the surgery had a successful outcome even if the patient is still not able to return to work. It's easy to imagine similar situations. Take, for example, the use of orthoscopic surgery. If it takes 25 operations for a surgeon to become proficient at orthoscopic surgery, do you want to be number 11? Does every physician perform at the same level of proficiency? Of course not.

Nowhere is this debate over quality more evident than in the area of open-heart surgery. It has become the status symbol on which hospitals hang their reputation. But not all bypasses are grafted equally. The evidence suggests that for patients, the choice of a hospital for heart surgery can literally be a matter of life or death. In 1985, the state of Arizona abandoned its program for allowing open-heart surgery only at certified medical centers. At the time, four hospitals had open heart programs.

Soon after deregulation, seven other hospitals began open heart programs. What happened? In the first year after deregulation, the mortality rate for open heart surgery soared by 35 percent. Nor did deregulation result in lower prices through increased competition. In fact, the average cost rose more than 50 percent.

What happened in Arizona is the proof of an obvious truth: You only get good at something with practice. Be it open heart surgery or golf, the more you do it, the better you become. Yet, in the United States, of the 850 hospitals that perform open heart surgery, only 375 do at least 250 operations in a given year. About 100 hospitals do fewer than 50 operations a year. But don't expect these hospitals to tell you who they are. They know this will scare away customers. Nor should you expect the doctor to tell you that he's never done a knee replacement.

Why is this information so hard to come by? In practically every other product or service sold in the open market, the consumer can find out some basic measures by which to judge one vendor from the other. But in medicine, as we have seen, it's hard to obtain any information about the effectiveness of various procedures, let alone of various practitioners. The routine coverup of unsuccessful procedures by the medical fraternity is notorious. The closest the consumer can come to judging quality in medical care is when the Health Care Financing Administration (HCFA) publishes, by hospital, the mortality rate of Medicare patients. Naturally, the hospitals hate it, especially when they come out looking worse than their counterparts.

In 1992, the *Wall Street Journal* published a lengthy article about one subset of statistics HCFA keeps, regarding the disparity in the mortality rate of patients having open heart surgery at two hospitals in Pennsylvania. In the course of the article, the administrators of the hospital with a worse-than-to-be-expected mortality rate trotted out the standard jargon about why medical statistics should not be made available to the public: Medicine is too complicated for the public to interpret. In a related defense, doctors told the newspaper that if mortality rates of heart surgeons were published, doctors would start refusing to treat sicker patients in order to improve their statistics. The reporters writing the story didn't buy it. First, as they pointed out, there are programs that adjust survival statistics to account for the difference in the condition of patients. Moreover, they quoted the federal judge who dismissed the "medicine is too complicated" defense en route to ordering the state of New York to release the patient mortality rates of heart surgeons to the Long Island *Newsday*.

The medical establishment in New York had fought release of this information tooth and nail. Why? Because physicians are used to practicing without being accountable. Why would any rational person want to change a system where everyone gets paid roughly the same (you know, "usual and customary") regardless of ability, regardless of "outcome?" If the medical community wanted information on quality they could easily have it. But instead they retreat to the ethical principal that a doctor should never question the professional judgment of a colleague. How deeply ingrained is this principal? Go back and look at the founding articles of the American Medical Association when it was formed in 1847. There it is: One of the first canons of ethics promulgated—no practitioner should question the medical decision of another practitioner.

All of this is not an exercise in AMA bashing. As we shall see, it gets to the heart of what's wrong with our medical system. Conversely, introducing true quality distinctions about medicine into the public domain is one of the keys to unraveling the mess our health care system is in.

SUPREME COURT ALBANY COUNTY,
SPECIAL TERM , AUGUST 9, 1991
JUSTICE HAROLD J. HUGHES,
PRESIDING

HUGHES, J. :
The petition will be granted:
*...the State [argued that] it must protect its citizens from their intellectual shortcomings by keeping from them information beyond their ability to comprehend.... Even if there was a legitimate privacy expectation, the interest of the public outweighs it. The Department of Health recognized such by releasing the information to the hospitals so that patients, as consumers, could make a more intelligent decision about which cardiac surgeons to choose. The same **public interest compels that the information be made available to** the rest of the State. Submit judgment.*
Dated October 15, 1991

SO WHAT ARE THE FACTS?

a. In 1986, how many more spinal fusions were performed on patients in the western U.S. than in the northeastern U.S.?

b. How much did the U.S. pay for fraudulent health insurance billing in 1991?

c. In 1992 what percent of diagnostic imaging centers in the state of Florida was owned by physicians?

Answers:

a. 9 times more

b. $50-$100 Billion

c. 93%

CHAPTER 5:
HOW TO BECOME
A SELF-MADE
(MEDICAL)
MILLIONAIRE

Health Images Inc. operates a chain of diagnostic imaging centers. This company initially formed partnerships with doctors in its locale to raise capital and get started. Over time, the company decided that it was not to its advantage to continue keeping doctors as partners. After purchasing the physicians' interest in one particular joint venture, company officials reviewed patient charts to check the number of negative scans performed. Negative scans are tests showing that nothing was wrong, such as an X-ray indicating that the patient with the hurt finger didn't have a broken bone. On the average, the percentage of negative scans at diagnostic centers operated by Health Images was about 25 percent.

But at this particular center, which was jointly owned with the physicians, there were twice as many negative scans. The company subsequently told a congressional subcommittee that the evidence suggested "that many patients were being referred for unnecessary procedures."

Unnecessary procedures, it should be noted, that made money for the providers who referred their patients to the center. It seems unlikely that these doctors, who happened to be co-owners of this imaging center, were all such poor diagnosticians that they needed the benefit of these tests to verify clinical judgments. Or is it possible that these providers, having absolute control over how much medical care the patient received, were ordering "just in case" procedures under the justifications that "more is better" or "I might be sued" or "I happen to have three kids in college," or all of the above. The theme is familiar. Who's it going to hurt? Insurance pays for it, right?

Surely those who answer the honorable calling to a career healing the sick would not be so crass, so petty, as to knowingly order needless tests because it will make them more money. Or would they?

In fact, many of our health care providers — maybe most, no one really knows — are emphatically NOT so crass and petty as to knowingly bilk their patients or their insurance companies by ordering needless tests at clinics in which they have a financial interest.

But it does happen. The AMA admits it — as evidenced by its advice discouraging self-referrals under its ethical guidelines. But guidelines are made to be broken, as the AMA incredibly demonstrated in the summer of 1992.

During its convention that year, the AMA's House of Delegates — its policy-making body of 434 doctors — actually voted to ENDORSE letting doctors own labs and refer patients to them. How could the AMA so blatantly and publicly (for it was widely reported) flaunt its own previously announced ethical standards? Chalk it up to a massive, institutional fit of pique. Asked to explain itself, one AMA trustee told the *Wall Street Journal* that the vote was "a clear expression of frustration" by doctors angry at increasing pressure from government against their owning labs to which they refer patients.

Of course, this wasn't the official reason the AMA cited in its remarkable contradiction. Rather, it said it was endorsing an exception to its guidelines against self-referral on the grounds that some patients might be harmed by an absolute policy against self referral, and because not that many doctors abuse the process.

The evidence, though, seems to be entirely to the contrary.

In 1985 the University of Arizona studied the insurance claims of 65,000 patients. It found that doctors with imaging equipment in offices owned by them ordered FOUR times as many tests as those who referred patients elsewhere.

In Florida, the problem of self-referrals became so widespread that the state Health Care Cost Containment Board spent months investigating the phenomenon while preparing what became a three volume report released in the fall of

1991. It found that doctors owned 93 percent of all diagnostic imaging centers in the state. In fact, according to a study by the University of Florida, 40 percent of all doctors in Florida have financial interests in medical facilities. And, in findings similar to the Arizona study, researchers for the advocacy group Public Citizen found that in Florida, there were twice as many tests per patient in doctor-owned labs as there were at independently owned labs.

Need more evidence? In California, a private study by William M. Mercer Inc. of 6,500 workers compensation claims found that 76 percent of all referrals to three types of outpatient facilities — physical therapy centers, MRI/CAT scan centers, and psychiatric treatment centers — were made by doctors who had a financial interest in these facilities. The study found one-third of all charges at these centers to be excessive or unnecessary. Consider also a national study in 1989 by the Department of Health and Human Services. It found that 27 percent of all physical therapy centers, 25 percent of all clinical labs, and 8 percent of medical surgery centers were owned entirely or in part by doctors. Patients of doctors who referred patients to facilities in which they had a financial interest received 46 percent more services than other patients.

Finally, consider the evidence of just one new cottage industry spawned by the trend toward self-referrals. In the early 1980's, a new company called T^2 got off the ground by offering "infusion therapy" — intravenous feeding and medication — for patients at home. The company's sure-fire strategy involved getting a group of doctors in a given area to invest in a center. Typically, the doctors referred their patients to the center and the company collected a management fee. Once the center was up and running, the company would then buy out the doctors, paying them in shares of T^2 stock. Then, as a result, the doctors retained a financial interest in the company and would continue referring their patients to the center. The concept was so lucrative that very quickly T^2 grew to 109 centers and was managing another 100.

Many doctors are aware of the black eye that physicians are very publicly inflicting on themselves through what appears to the public to be unmitigated greed. Chief among them is Arnold Relman, the former editor-in-chief of the *New England Journal of Medicine*. In testifying to the Health Care Cost Containment board in Florida, he said that doctors who send patients to facilities they own have a conflict of interest that would not be tolerated anywhere in the business world. As for the argument that doctors can act in the best interest of their patients and ignore the fact that they'll profit from whatever tests they have their patients undergo, Relman said, "On the face of it, it's ridiculous."

Another doctor, James Schwade of the Radiation Oncology Department at the University of Miami, put the practice of self-referral in even more blunt terms for a congressional subcommittee: "No matter how it is structured, conceived, or concealed, it is what it is: a kickback."

Schwade's comment gets to the heart of the matter, for what is at issue is not the doctors' ethics but our finances. The costs of all these excess and unnecessary tests add up and are tacked on to our national health bill. In Florida alone, the cost of unnecessary procedures has been estimated at $500 million a year, a tab so steep that in 1992 the Florida legislature bucked the medical lobby and passed a law that bars doctors from investing in medical labs. In doing this, Florida was following the example set by the anti-self-referral laws passed, or proposed, in Michigan, Maryland, New Jersey, California, and Minnesota. These efforts are a start. And Congress, after hearings on self-referral, wrote a ban on self-referral into the 1994 Medicare and Medicaid budget. But the ban is so full of holes — it cites 15 exceptions — that it essentially has no teeth. And until we have something more effective (and that covers all patients, not just those on Medicare and Medicaid), we all will bear the cost through higher insurance premiums that finance unnecessary procedures that fatten the bottom-line for physician-owned facilities.

PSSSST! HEY, BUDDY, WANNA MAKE SOME DOUGH?

(A letter entered into evidence before the House Ways and Means Committee hearing, Oct. 17, 1991 sic!)

Dear Dr. Cress:

If you are typical of the doctors we talk with, you have probably noticed a marked decline in your income during the last year or so. We are also sure that you are as familiar as we are with the reasons why this has occurred. With the increase in competition within the medical field, changes in Medicare and Medicaid reimbursements, cuts in private insurance payments, and workers compensation payments being reduced by the insurance companies, this situation is not going to get any better.

More important and to the point, as an orthopedic surgeon there is something you can do about it! We know your first priority is to provide the finest care possible to your patients! If you would like to know how you can provide this standard of care for your patients that need physical therapy and receive an additional thirty to fifty thousand dollars a year that you have been sending to your competition, that's right, your competition, read on. The American Physical Therapy Association has been actively campaigning to allow physical therapists to treat patients without a doctors prescription! Fortunately, this aggressive approach to interfering with the doctor-patient relationship has not yet been approved in all states, but twenty-one states have approved it or have it under consideration.

We at National Physical Therapy Management Inc. don't believe that physical therapists should be allowed to practice medicine. We don't believe that this is good for the patient, good for the doctor, or even good for the physical therapists and we do not allow patients to be treated at any of the clinics with which we are affiliated without a prescription from a licensed physician. Dr. Cress, physician owned therapy clinics are nothing new. If you are not referring your patients to your own clinic, you may already be referring them unknowingly to another physician-owned clinic, with all the attendant disadvantages. By the way, your participation in a business venture structured as these physical therapy clinics are organized will not conflict with the Medical Practice Act of any state or compromise the ethics of your profession.

As the saying goes, "You can lead a horse to water but you can't make him drink." If, at this point, you are still not interested in adding $30,000 to $50,000 a year (that's $2500.00 to $4000.00 a month) to your personal income, there is not much else we can say. Except, you probably don't have enough information to make a rational decision. In closing however, we will leave you with this thought: You are probably in the 38.5% marginal income tax bracket, which means that out of every dollar you earn, you must pay almost forty cents in taxes. The profits that you would earn as a partner in your own physical therapy clinic would be passive income and, as such, could be offset by any passive losses you may have incurred from other past investment activities.

This, in effect, amounts to Legitimate Tax Free Income. Check it out with your accountant, if you like... and return the enclosed card for additional information and let us show you how we can have your clinic in operation in ninety days or less.

Sincerely, John Marr, Director of Clinic Development

SO WHAT ARE THE FACTS?

a. How much did the U.S. spend on health care in 1987, 1989, 1991, 1993?

b. How much did Canada spend on health care in 1987, 1989, 1991, 1993?

c. In 1992 how much did the AARP *net* from administering group health insurance?

d. How much did AARP *gross* from membership dues?

e. Approximately what percentage of AARP 1992 net Operating Revenues came from administering health care insurance?

Answers:

a. In 1987, $494 Billion
In 1989, $603 Billion
In 1991, $751 Billion
In 1993 (est.) $1.0 Trillion.
A 15% annual rate of inflation, more than three times the general rate of inflation.

b. 1987 $48.7 Billion (Canadian) *
1989 $57.8 Billion
1991 $67.2 Billion
1993 (est) $77 Billion
An annual inflation rate of over 15%.

* Canada's population (ca. 26 million) is approximately 1/10th that of the U.S. (ca. 248 million).

c. The AARP netted $84,099,000 from administering health care insurance.

d. The AARP grossed $102,211,000 from membership dues.

e. Approximately 82% of AARP's 1992 net operating revenues came from administering health care insurance.

CHAPTER 6:
THE REAL CULPRIT

What is bedeviling our health care system? Previously we examined the commonly advanced reasons for why our medical costs are spiraling out of control — the proliferation of technology, the aging population, red tape, defensive medicine, malpractice, drugs, unbundling and cost shifting. These are all symptoms of the disease, but they are not the disease itself. That's why so-called fixes advanced by various parties to reform our health care system are doomed to fail. ANY health reform plan we adopt, EVEN A SINGLE PAYER CANADIAN-STYLE PLAN, is going to fail if we measure it against the only yardstick that counts: How well will it control medical spending?

It is true that Canada spent about $2,000 per person for health care in 1991, while the United States spent about $3,000. But it is also true, as the insurance lobby points out in fighting to save its existence by making sure we don't adopt a Canadian-style system, that THE COST OF MEDICINE IN CANADA IS RISING PROPORTIONALLY JUST AS FAST AS IT IS IN THE UNITED STATES.

So what is the disease? What is the real culprit? It's our system itself. Start with the physician who generates 80 percent of the demand (and thus the costs) for medical services. Then give him a seemingly magic pocket called "third-party pay" in which he can dip endlessly for money. Add to this the fact that the insurance is paid for by an employer or the government, not the patient (who couldn't care less about what the costs happen to be.)

The obvious falls into place. You get exactly what we have: A proliferation of subspecialists, ordering bushel baskets of tests under a "more is better" approach, having oodles of defensive justifications and rationalizations to keep piling it on. Providers can generate unlimited demand for services under a fee-for-service arrangement, and providers also know that the third party magic called insurance, workers' compensation, Medicaid and Medicare will pay.

Unfortunately, the matter is compounded by some unscrupulous physicians — and even some scrupulous ones who kid themselves that they're doing what's best for the patient — ordering needless tests (some at clinics they own) because they know they will get paid and that the patient is not going to fuss, because the patient is not paying the bill.

This greatly flawed foundation has led to the mansion of maladies afflicting our health care system: The skyrocketing insurance rates, the 37 million people without health insurance, the proliferation of paperwork that seems to grow geometrically as the market place attempts to find ways to restrain medical spending.

It's time to change our health-care system before it bankrupts our society. Don't think that this is some melodramatic exaggeration. If we don't change our health care system, we will bankrupt our society and soon. In 1960, we spent 4.4 percent of our Gross National Product on health care. In 1992, we spent 14.0 percent, and by the year 2000, if nothing changes, it will be 18 percent or 1.5 TRILLION dollars. Up and up. That's 18 percent of our money that doesn't do a thing to increase national wealth. It doesn't build roads or bridges, it doesn't finance research for new consumer products that we can manufacture and sell to consumers at home or in other countries. It doesn't give us better schools — we can't even invest it and earn interest on the money. This senseless level of spending may buy good health for some, but at the rate we are going we will end up the healthiest impoverished nation in history.

The real culprit is the system, which is built on a set of economic incentives that, when confronted by any rational person, increase health costs as relentlessly as the incoming tide.

The solution to what ails our health care system is not incredibly complex. In fact, contrary to much of the debate you hear about health care reform, we do not need to dismantle our health care system and rebuild it from scratch. The fact is, with some small but fundamental adjustments we could leave our current system intact and let a new set of economic incentives work to contain medical costs.

But first, to understand why this simple solution — which I will detail in Section 3 — would work, we must examine how we came to be in the mess we're in. So let's pause to examine how our health care system evolved into a monster feeding from what I call The Magic Pockets.

MONEY TALKS

When it comes down to doing right by themselves or by the country, it's easy to see where the medical industry stands. Just look where they put their money.

During the 1980's, they put $60 million of it directly into the hands of congressmen and senators, according to a Common Cause study of more than 200 medical industry PACs published in 1992. (God knows what the indirect payments were.)

Forty percent of this went to members of the four committees that oversee health-related issues. And the PACs were arrogantly candid with Common Cause about what they want for this investment. **"We spend our money on those members most interested in maintaining the current system,"** said Tom Goodwill, a spokesman for the America Federation of Health Systems, which represents 1,400 for-profit hospitals.

Is it any wonder that health reform, so obviously needed for so many years, went nowhere for so long?

Section 2:

How Did We Get Here? The Rise Of The Magic Pockets

SO WHAT ARE THE FACTS?

Of the 55 independent Blue Cross/Blue Shield plans in the U.S. which were rated in 1992 on claims-paying ability, how many were rated in each of the following categories?

Category A, highest 20%
Category B, next 20%
Category C, next 20%
Category D, next 20%
Category F, lowest 20%

Answers:
A Highest   2
B   23
C   21
D   2
F Lowest   7
An overall rating of C-.

CHAPTER 7:
THE BIRTH OF THE BLUES:
THE FIRST MAGIC POCKET

Most people don't realize that the concept of pre-paid insurance for health care is the nucleus of the economic bonanza enjoyed by the health care establishment. Pre-paid insurance has made health care the largest industry IN THE WORLD.

In 1992 the United States alone spent more than $850 billion — BILLION — for health care. As we have seen, the health-insurance industry has been growing by leaps and bounds for years. Yet, it is a concept born of desperation.

The concept of insurance — pre-payments to spread risk, to absorb the cost of catastrophic occurrences — has been around for centuries. Ancient Romans in the shipping business had insurance to guard against the loss of a cargo at sea. But before 1932, the generally agreed upon start of the Blue Cross system of pre-paid health insurance, health care was not widely insured. Health care was provided, in fact, like any other business. Like any other business, the patient paid for the services received. And like any other business, when cash was not available some other compensation, perhaps a pig or a bushel of tomatoes, might be offered. And like any other business, the provider, the doctor, had to decide (if the patient could not pay cash) whether or not to accept the pig or the tomatoes or quite possibly provide the service (heaven forbid) for free. Before things reached this stage, of course, the doctor had to look the patient in the eye and tell the poor soul just how much the services would cost and justify the value. Finally, just like any other business, the doctor might ultimately choose to charge a reduced fee if his performance was not up to par and he wanted to keep the patient as a customer. All of these components of the free enterprise system once applied to health care. (It should be noted, however, that even then doctors' incomes were about six times higher than those of the average worker.)

What happened to change all of this? There are many reasons for the change, but a very major contributor is the birth of the Blues: Blue Cross and Blue Shield. These two institutions were conceived out of financial necessity resulting from the economic drought of the Great Depression. The original Blue Cross system was, quite simply, a way to enable people to have hospital care when they were sick by having paid for hospitalization in advance, at a time when they were healthy.

Why did hospitals flock to Blue Cross? Because during the Depression people were not using hospitals — they had little money to spend. Hospitals all over the country were going out of business; they faced a crisis that threatened their very existence.

But the solution to this crisis was at hand. In fact, it had already been tested and proven successful, in Texas, at Baylor University Hospital in Dallas. Starting in 1929, the administrators at Baylor used an innovative program that became the model for Blue Cross associations throughout the country. In the late 1920's, Baylor found itself in the same position that all hospitals would soon face as the Depression gripped the nation — it had rows of empty beds, and no cash flow. So Baylor began offering a pre-paid hospital plan to school teachers in Dallas. For 50 cents a month, subscribers could receive up to 21 days of care in the hospital every year. It was a stroke of genius. It gave the hospitals a steady source of cash at a time of economic uncertainty, and it gave patients assurance that if they became seriously ill, they would be able to go to the hospital. It had advantages for all concerned.

The first Blue Cross Association, copying the Baylor model, was started in 1932 in Sacramento, California. The concept spread rapidly across the country. If fact, Blue Cross proved so successful that by the late 1930's, doctors adapted this system for themselves, under the name Blue Shield. Blue Shield worked much the same way as Blue Cross. Subscribers were entitled to a doctor's services in return for prepaying a monthly fee. When Blue Cross and Blue Shield ultimately merged in 1962, a force was born that was to alter the history of health care in the United States.

Why did Blue Cross/Blue Shield sweep across the country in just a few years? Part of the answer, as we have seen, lies in the obvious economic advantage to both patients and providers. But for the providers — the ones who actually started the system — there was a secondary benefit of enormous appeal. Blue Cross/Blue Shield essentially became the marketing arm for physicians and hospitals. With this new organization in place, physicians could sell medical services directly to consumers without having to tarnish their professional reputations, and their self-esteem, by stooping to use that unseemly practice of marketing.

Although there were variations of the Blue Cross/Baylor concept before 1929, they had not become legitimate business enterprises for one simple reason: There was no economic imperative to bring people into this system. Historically people could pay for and obtain health care on their own. Consumers were in control of their own choices, just as they are in control of their choices today for auto insurance, home owners insurance, and life insurance (sister products to health insurance), which have not experienced the same massive escalation in costs.

En route to becoming the dominant force in medical insurance, Blue Cross/Blue Shield managed to get an important break that became one of the fundamental seeds of today's cost crisis. As a non-profit organization, Blue Cross successfully lobbied state legislators into being considered separate from other types of insurance. Other insurance, such as life, homeowners, or auto coverage, is indemnification based. In return for a certain level of premium, the customer receives a certain level of reimbursement or benefits in the event of a loss, and no more.

But Blue Cross/Blue Shield did not operate this way. They didn't provide reimbursement in the event of poor health, they provided services; whatever services it took to get patients back to good health. Because of the humanitarian nature of the enterprise, and because they were non-profit, the regulators exempted Blue Cross/Blue Shield from having to maintain the same large cash reserves to absorb unexpectedly large claims.

Other insurance companies saw the explosive growth in Blue Cross/Blue Shield and decided to get into the health-insurance business, too. They found that to be competitive, they had to model their programs on those offered by Blue Cross, i.e. medical services in return for premiums. More-over, they too were exempted from having to carry large reserves.

The upshot of all this, sixty years later, is that health insurance companies must pay for health care services racked up by their subscribers in a given year out of that year's premiums. Remember there are no reserves, so when costs go up 10 percent or more a year, as they have for almost two decades, it follows that health insurance premiums are also going to increase that much or more the next year. And it doesn't matter if you don't go to the hospital or the doctor all year. You are still part of the pool of people to whom the policy is sold. If anyone in the pool goes to the doctor or hospital that year, which is a virtual certainty, then the premiums for everyone in the pool will go up. In the Blue Cross/Blue Shield system there was a hidden phenomenon at work, a phenomenon that was born out of a seemingly ethical motivation but which became the demon seed.

Let's take a moment to review the facts. Who is Blue Cross/Blue Shield's customer? The answer seems obvious. It is, of course the patient, or at least the corporate employer, who writes the check every month to pay the bill for the patient's insurance coverage. Right? Wrong! The basic philosophy of the Blue Cross system— at least, as it was founded — was that doctors would have majority control of the board of directors and that the insurance company will never tell the doctors how to practice medicine. At least one legitimate philosophical platitude did emerge — let's reserve the medical decision-making to those with the professional license. But the result was that the real customer for Blue Cross/Blue Shield is not the patient but the doctor — the logical relationship, given that the health insurance company had become the marketing arm for physicians. As the medical marketing arm, there is no other way to view the physician except as the customer: Doctors established the organization; doctors controlled the board. And after all, who is it that fills the hospital beds? Do patients check themselves in?

EVEN DOCTORS GET THE BLUES

The establishment of Blue Cross/Blue Shield by medical providers has had lasting and financially damaging ramifications for our society. As an organization that was totally controlled, literally, by medical providers, Blue Cross/Blue Shield was created with one orientation: To make people better after they get sick. This, after all, is what doctors and hospitals do. It's what they get paid for. They are not paid to prevent disease and teach people how to keep themselves healthy, or how to attend to the 50 percent or more of the ailments that people could treat without medical help if they knew what to do.

Since treatment costs far more than prevention, this orientation increased our collective health bill, but Blue Cross/Blue Shield didn't mind. After all, they receive a percentage of premiums. As health costs went up, premiums also went up. And as premiums went up, income went up. And because all commercial health insurance came to be modeled on the Blue Cross/Blue Shield model, all insurance companies came to love those annual premium increases that they passed on to their customers, chiefly the companies that provide health benefits for their employees.

But the health industry finally went too far: They pushed prices beyond what the market — the companies buying health care insurance for their employees — would bear. And when companies realized that it would cost them less to pay their employees' health bills out of pocket than to let the insurance companies stick it to them, they began dropping their policies. Today, 75 percent of the Fortune 500 companies are "self-insured," as this practice is called.

As the trend began spreading from the megacompanies to even moderate sized concerns, the insurance companies finally woke up to the danger. And now they are scrambling to realign themselves to meet the needs of their remaining customers — the real customers, the companies that pay the health premiums.

Even Blue Cross/Blue Shield, the last bastion, has begun to recognize the new reality. Slowly, the makeup of the Blue Cross/Blue Shield boards has changed so that doctors and hospitals no longer have total control. In some states, Blue Cross/Blue Shield even sets aside a seat or two for subscribers. So, while doctors still have a lot of influence, they are not the absolute dictators of health policy that they once were.

And at least one Blue Cross/Blue Shield president acknowledges that the influence that the medical professionals still retain will inevitably decrease. In her remarks at a conference in 1991, Phyllis Marstiller, the President of Blue Cross/Blue Shield of Virginia, said, "I am convinced that this change will be forced by the individual consumers and corporations of America, who pay the bulk of the health care bill in this country. **It is clear to me that the control of our health care system is rapidly shifting away from doctors and hospitals to the people who really pay the bill."**

SO WHAT ARE THE FACTS?

a. In 1930, how much was spent per capita on health care in the U.S.?

b. In 1993, what is the estimated per capita spending on health care in the U.S.?

c. What was the percentage increase in health care costs during the 1980's?

d. What percentage of medical services is emergency driven?

Answers:
a. $23
b. $4000
c. 117%
d. 15%

CHAPTER 8:
THE "BENEFITS" OF ORGANIZED LABOR: MORE THAN WE BARGAINED FOR

As we have seen previously, once upon a time medical services were provided like all other services in the free market. We paid directly for services received. The patient paid for the service received and the provider had to look the patient in the eye and discuss the cost.

The original Blue Cross system essentially kept this principal intact. While it was true that patients did not pay at the time they received the service, they did pay, through the premiums they sent in every month. But in the 1940's the fundamental principle of a free market system began to erode within our health care system.

The erosion began during World War II, when there was a shortage of workers to run the factories at home. To keep the laws of supply and demand from escalating wages at a time when the nation could ill afford it, the federal government imposed a wage freeze on the country. The War Labor Board did, however, allow management to include health insurance as a workplace benefit. And the IRS allowed the benefit to be deducted as a cost of doing business. Given the wartime tax rates, companies were only too happy to embrace a new benefit that kept their employees happy while reducing their tax liability. And the employees, with their health insurance premiums now being paid, received a de facto wage increase since they now could buy other things with the money they saved.

It didn't take long for organized labor to realize what a good deal this was, and some unions began demanding that companies pay their health-insurance premiums. Business resisted, but lost the battle when, in 1948, the National Labor Relations Board ruled that health benefits were legitimate grounds for conducting a strike. Management appealed but in 1949 the Supreme Court upheld the NLRB. These twin rulings were to tilt our health care system far away from the tradition of the market economy. Soon, unions began to demand health insurance as part of the employment package, and companies easily agreed since (at the time) the cost was insignificant, and it was tax deductible. In due time, this became the norm for businesses, so even non-unionized companies offered health benefits as the industry standard. No company of any size could compete for quality workers without offering these benefits.

This direction led to one of the most significant problems with our medical system. The overwhelming majority of Americans with health insurance get their insurance through their employer. For all but a handful, this insurance is not portable. We can't take our policy with us if we change jobs. Consequently, there's a new term that crops up in health care: "job lock." That's when people are locked into their jobs because if they quit, they cannot get new insurance coverage due to a pre-existing medical condition. The reason for this situation has to do with the way insurance works, and it also reveals why the system of obtaining health care coverage through employers has had a profound effect on the way insurance companies do business.

Typically, insurance premiums for any type of insurance are based on the claims experience of the group that is insured— the pool. For auto insurance, consumers are in a pool comprised of themselves and other individuals of like age, geographical range, and driving history. Everyone in the pool shares the cost of the accidents caused by all members of the pool. If the members of the pool have a bad year, premiums go up for everyone in the pool.

When it comes to health insurance, the pool most often is the employees of a group of companies. Health insurance premiums are based on the health costs of the group. Some businesses, of course, are more dangerous than others, and so they have more accidents and higher medical costs.

Now, let's take a look at who is actually paying the medical bills. Initially, it was Blue Cross. It paid the bills, then split the costs among the companies comprising the pool and raised their premiums accordingly each year if cost went up. But, as other insurance companies began to compete with Blue Cross, they realized that as competitors they could offer lower rates if they only dealt with those companies having a history of low claims. Soon insurance companies became ever more creative in defining pools so they could lure away the business of the healthiest (and most profitable) people. In the industry, this is known as "cherry-picking." And cherry-picking undermines the principal of shared risk that is the bedrock of the industry.

Here's a simplified example: Suppose there are 10 people in the pool. Nine are healthy and have annual medical expenses of $100 each. One person has a chronic condition and has annual medical bills of about $4,000. To cover the medical costs of everyone in the pool, each member pays a $500 premium. But what happens if a competitor takes the nine healthy people out of the pool and puts them in a new low-risk pool? The premiums these nine pay drop dramatically. But the person with the chronic condition ends up (if he can get insurance at all) in a high-risk pool with other people who have high medical bills. His premiums skyrocket. This is what insurance companies have done by cherry picking. The high-risk businesses (that is, businesses prone to accidents) have seen their premiums rise so high that many of them have had to drop health benefits for their employees entirely. That's why two-thirds of the uninsured in this country are workers or their dependents.

Now go back to the concept of job lock and determine why it is happening. Let's say you are an accountant and you want to change jobs. You are pretty healthy, except for a kidney problem. You were born with only one good kidney, and this good one has been getting less and less efficient as you have aged. Now you're 42 and the doctor says your good kidney has failed entirely, leaving you dependent on dialysis. You may be a candidate for a transplant. Your present company's health plan has covered your dialysis costs because you've been with them for 19 years, well before it was discovered that your good kidney had failed. A new company is eager to hire you at a higher salary, but there's a catch: Their health insurance won't cover your kidney problem. The reason is simply that if they did, the costs would be so high that the insurance company would have to raise the premiums significantly to your employer and the other employers in the pool it had lured from Blue Cross by offering the lower premiums. So you stay with your old company, because there's no way you can afford to deal with your kidney condition out of your own pocket. You are locked into your job.

Job lock affects not only people with medical problems, but people having family members with medical problems. The problem is not rare. A 1991 study in New York estimated that 20 percent of that state's workers were affected by job lock. It's one consequence of getting health insurance through an employer.

However, there is a much more insidious, but rarely mentioned, effect of the influence of organized labor in health care. It goes to the very heart of what ails our system. When business took over the responsibility for paying employees' health insurance premiums, they added a layer of bureaucracy that insulated the employees from the real cost of care. No longer was the person who received the service paying the bill.

Human nature quickly took over. If it doesn't cost me anything, give me the best and the most. The recipient of the benefit had no incentive but to take, take, and take some more. The recipient of the benefit did not care what it cost. The providers of the service had no incentive but to give, give, give, and they too did not care about the cost because they didn't have to confront patients with such an "unseemly" issue as money.

No one foresaw these consequences when health insurance evolved from being an individual responsibility to a workplace benefit. But now that the system has run its course for 40 years, the deleterious effects are all too clear.

Many companies have adopted measures to control health costs: copayments, deductibles, and HMO's. But unions have fought efforts to apply these measures to employees. As one AFL-CIO official said, "Workers do not want to be the payers of last resort." We have achieved a full-entitlement mentality with runaway demand in the hands of providers who benefit from these excesses.

HEALTH CARE OR BUST!

Unsuspecting members of the public who didn't realize just how important unions have come to view their health benefits were jolted to reality in April, 1991 when the railroad unions staged a national strike over, among, other things, management's insistence that union members bear, for the first time, some portion of the cost of their health insurance. The strike followed a year of unsuccessful efforts by a presidential mediation board to get the railroads and their workers to settle on a new contract that would include some health cost sharing. At stake was the very economic viability of the nation: railroads accounted or 37 percent of all the inter-city freight moved in the country, 60 percent of the coal, 67 percent of the automobiles, 68 percent of pulp and paper products, 53 percent of the lumber, 53 percent of the chemicals, and 45 percent of the food.

On April 17, after neither side would accept the presidential board's recommendations, the picket lines went up, but not for long. As with previous strikes, Congress stepped in immediately. The House passed special legislation late that night imposing the board's recommendations. The Senate forwarded the bill without a vote to President Bush, who was awakened at 1:38 in the morning to sign the bill.

The importance of health benefits in the strike should not have come as a surprise to anyone who had followed the evolving nature of labor negotiations throughout the 1980s. During that decade, as health costs began to soar, management began seeing its profits squeezed and began asking workers to pay a portion of their health insurance premiums. The workers typically resisted, and strikes sometimes resulted. **By 1989, a survey by the Metropolitan Life Insurance Co. found that half of the labor leaders surveyed said that fighting cost-sharing on health benefits was more important than winning higher wages.**

SO WHAT ARE THE FACTS?

a. In 1980, what percent of the federal budget was spent on Medicare and Medicaid?

b. In 1992, what percent of the federal budget was spent on Medicare and Medicaid?

c. During what decade did physician's incomes double?

d. Prior to 1966, who were originally the most active opponents of Medicare and Medicaid?

Answers:

a. 10%

b. 15%

c. The 1960's

d. The AMA and The American Hospital Association

CHAPTER 9:
THE GREAT SOCIETY GETS GREATER AND GREATER: MAGIC POCKETS TWO AND THREE

If ever there was a magic (and deep) pocket for health care providers, it is Medicare and Medicaid.

Although the federal government is now making serious efforts to rein in costs, in the beginning — and for many years thereafter — these federal programs were the physician's best friend. They were a veritable national bank in the waiting room. They let providers set their own fees and collect as much as desired, all in the noble name of treating the aged and the poor.

Why did the government give physicians this carte blanche, this system that amounted to letting physicians write unlimited purchase orders for the government to pay?

As you might guess, politics and interest groups, and not least, the AMA, had a lot to do with it. It is one of the great ironies of the 20th century that for years the AMA fought Medicare.

The impulse to provide health care for the elderly dates back to the 1940's, when proposals abounded to add a health care component to Social Security. These proposals, which the AMA opposed vigorously, did not succeed; but in 1951 they enjoyed a brief resurgence when President Truman shifted his position from advocating universal health care for all Americans to federal government-subsidized hospital insurance for the elderly.

This idea was short-lived, though, because President Eisenhower, who succeeded Truman in 1952, was happy with things as they were. Congress, however, was still interested in the issue and held hearings during the 1950's on the subject. Of course, behind this interest lay a political agenda: As advances in medicine lengthened life spans, more and more people were reaching old age only to find that they could not afford medical care. Thus, there was a ground swell of opinion that something should be done to address this problem. But more to the point, with the increasing life spans came a corresponding rise in the proportion of the voting-age population that was over 65. By 1965, the population over 65 would account for about 10 percent of the voters — a constituency too large to be ignored by the politicians.

During these hearings, much of the discussion centered on how health care for the elderly should be implemented. There were two schools of thought. One school said that the government should remove the stigma of public assistance by giving health benefits to all the elderly, regardless of their financial means. The other favored creating a new class of people deserving benefits only because of their financial inability to pay.

The first effort at actually implementing health care for the elderly came in 1957, when Senator Aimé Forand introduced a bill amending Social Security to include hospital and nursing home care for everyone, irrespective of financial status.

Forand's bill, fought by insurance companies and the AMA, died in committee. But, by 1960 it was clear that something had to be done. Rising health costs were pricing the aged out of the market and the issue became a political imperative.

Out of this came the Kerr-Mills Act of 1960, designed to address the problem by building on existing state programs for helping the elderly pay their medical bills. In concept, Kerr-Mills would solve the problem by having the federal government match 50 to 80 percent of state expenditures for the elderly population.

The problem was that actual state spending varied widely, so that vast inequities existed in the level of health care from one state to the another. In certain cases, such as 1961 in Georgia and 1964 in Mississippi, some states did not help the elderly at all because they couldn't afford to, so they received no Kerr-Mills matching funds from the federal government. Kerr-Mills also required that the elderly spend down their life savings before receiving benefits, and this proved to be very unpopular with the voters. Soon, Kerr-Mills was seen to be a hollow triumph for the elderly, despite the hyperbole in the press releases when the act was passed.

Most significantly, Kerr-Mills contained no provisions for limiting federal outlays for the program, either in the total amount spent for an individual patient or the total amount sent to each state. This oversight would come back to haunt the federal government.

As early as 1961, the inadequacies of Kerr-Mills were apparent enough that in his message to Congress that year, President Kennedy proposed amending Social Security to provide health care for the elderly. Through allies in Congress, Kennedy introduced a bill to that effect, but again, with the AMA and the insurance companies lobbying hard against it, the bill was bottled up in committee.

The Democratic landslide of 1964 finally broke the logjam. With the changed composition of the key committees, the Medicare proposal, now championed by President Johnson, started moving forward. Again the AMA moved in to fight. In testimony to Congress in 1965, Dr. Donovan Ward, the president of the AMA, could not have known that his words would have a completely different context in 1994: "We physicians care for the elderly and know their health needs better than anyone else," he said. "Having the government intrude into health care would not be good medicine."

As the debate about Medicare raged, other proposals were introduced into the mix: Senator Jacob Javits essentially wanted to expand Kerr-Mills and increase federal assistance to the states for caring for the poor and elderly. The AMA favored a plan that would have the federal and state government subsidize insurance premiums for the elderly. (i.e., Let's expand Blue Shield!)

Which plan won? They all did. What we call Medicare became the proverbial horse designed by a committee that ended up looking like a camel.

President Johnson, in order to get what he wanted, agreed to a bill that gave everybody else what they wanted. Javits got his plan through: It became Medicaid for the poor. And then Johnson got more of what he wanted: An expansion of Social Security to include hospital benefits and nursing home care. Because of its very mechanism — amending Social Security — the nation ended up with a health care program for all the elderly, not just those elderly in need. This is what we call today Medicare Part A.

Finally, the AMA got what it wanted: Its proposal for insurance subsidies became Medicare Part B, the program under which the federal government matches insurance premiums the elderly voluntarily pay to help cover doctor bills.

But, the AMA also got something more important: It got the government to agree that when doctors treated Medicare patients, they would be paid their "usual and customary" fees. And the more services they performed under their own fee schedules, the more they would get paid. No one was going to question the costs All doctors had to do was send in their bills and collect their checks. It was this concession that got the AMA on board, and it turned Medicare into the goose that laid the golden egg for the physicians.

Unfortunately, the government's agreement to pay the usual and customary fee was not the only way in which Medicare was designed to mimic private insurance. The program was deliberately structured to escape the damning accusation that it was "socialized medicine." In both administration and organization, Medicare was set up like private insurance. Like private insurance, it required deductibles and co-insurance, or additional payments once a certain level of benefits had been paid out. Even its basic services copied the insurance model, with Part A corresponding to Blue Cross and Part B to Blue Shield.

It didn't take long for the chickens to come home to roost. Medicaid was the first. Even as the legislation was in the process of being adopted, some states, notably California and New York, were positioning themselves to take full advantage of the matching funds opportunity. The upshot was that soon after Medicaid became law in 1965, Congress realized that it would cost far more than it expected. Instead of $200 million a year when fully implemented, it might be more like $3 billion a year. (What's a few billion if it means getting re-elected?) As to be expected, the government began retreating, and by 1967 the Congress passed the first of a series of bills that would restrict eligibility in an effort to restrain costs.

Medicare took longer to get into trouble. For the first nine years, costs increased steadily but not enough to panic Congress into tampering with the system. But by 1974, providers apparently had figured out how to use the system to their best advantage, and costs started soaring, from $10.7 billion in 1974 to $14.1 billion in 1975 to $20.8 billion in 1977 to $34 billion in 1980. Finally in 1983, Congress acted to halt the runaway growth in Medicare spending. It established a new system under which it would pay hospitals flat fees for given procedures, regardless of actual costs. It also slapped a 30-month freeze on payments to doctors, ending its practice of paying "usual and customary" fees — which, as we have seen, the doctors themselves had set.

These changes slowed but did not stop growth in spending as providers learned to work around the system. They began steering more and more patients into out-patient procedures, which were not covered under the new restrictions, and they began unbundling their charges. To control costs further, the government continued to impose more and more red tape and began limiting payments. Today, few doctors have much good to say about Medicare. And many independent clinics will no longer accept Medicare patients. Unwittingly, the physicians themselves killed the goose that laid their golden egg.

Our fling with an unchecked Medicare system has been costly for all of society. When the government slapped on price controls in the form of flat fees, hospitals and doctors didn't reduce their prices, they merely started shifting the unpaid cost to outpatient clinics and onto the privately insured population and the rise in medical spending in our country continues unabated.

DOCTORS' ORDERS
THE AMA AND HEALTH REFORM
THROUGH THE YEARS

One of the great ironies about the AMA's opposition to Medicare is that this program, and Medicaid, turned out to be one of the great wealth-generating machines for the medical industry.

Consider that in 1964, the year before Medicare and Medicaid was passed, the nation spent $38.1 billion on health care. By 1970, just five years after Congress created these programs, the national health bill was up to $74.4 billion. But in opposing Medicare and Medicaid, organized medicine was merely following its historic pattern of fighting any change in the status quo.

As early as 1920, the AMA was fighting early efforts in some states to establish compulsory health insurance for blue-collar workers; opponents called it a "German" scheme, which was about as nefarious an adjective as one could use in the years after World War I. In the late 1930s, the AMA dug in to put the Group Health Association, a fledgling managed-care organization, out of business. For its efforts, a grand jury indicted the AMA in 1939 for criminal conspiracy in restraint of trade and commerce. In 1943 the Supreme Court upheld lower court convictions, but the impact was negligible, because by then the AMA had made life so miserable for any doctor who dared join a group practice that no one did.

In the late 1940s, President Harry Truman wanted to institute national health insurance for all Americans. The AMA hired a public-relations company to orchestrate a campaign against the proposal, involving thousands of physicians, corporate heads, civic groups, and nonmedical trade associations, all decrying any change. The AMA won.

In 1962, President John Kennedy wanted to amend Social Security to include health care for the elderly. The AMA fight against Kennedy's proposal included "Operation Coffee Cup": doctors' wives invited friends and neighbors for a cup of coffee and to hear a tape of Ronald Reagan equating state-financed medical care for the elderly with the first step toward socialism.

The AMA won again. The one exception to this pattern of opposing reform has been when change was inevitable, such as in 1965, when passage of some sort of medical program for the elderly was inevitable. Then, the AMA sought to tailor reform to its needs by promoting an alternative to Medicare that it called "Eldercare." Now, once again, the AMA sees that health reform is a train that cannot be stopped. A headline in a 1991 issue of the Journal of the American Medical Association *sighed, "Health Reform: An aura of inevitability is upon us." So it is having state and local medical societies across the country "drop in" on newspapers and television stations to brief them on health reform.*

117

SO WHAT ARE THE FACTS?

a. In 1980, what was the average medical cost per workers' compensation claim?

b. In 1990, what was the average medical cost per workers' compensation claim?

c. What is the most common workers' compensation injury?

d. In 1991, what was the average cost per claim for a workers' compensation low back sprain?

Answers:
a. $1,748
b. $6,611
c. low back sprain
d. $23,916

CHAPTER 10:
THE WORKERS'
MIRACLE:
THE FOURTH MAGIC
POCKET

Now we've come to the fourth of the magic pockets, and in many respects, the most lucrative. It is the workers' compensation system. Many people do not think of workers' comp when they think about the components of our health care system. On the face of it, it seems more an industrial issue. Sure, a worker should be compensated when injured on the job, but what difference does it make to our health system if the injury is at home or at work? Well, it makes a lot of difference.

The workers' comp system dates back to 1911, when it was devised to address the growing problem of workplace injuries as our country industrialized. More and more employees were finding lawyers and medical experts willing to help them sue their employers over injuries, and these lawsuits were becoming a burden on everyone. Thus, the idea of a "no-fault" insurance system to cover medical costs for job injuries was created.

The system offered something for both sides. For the worker, the system guaranteed that medical costs would be covered, and they didn't have to pay the insurance premiums — the company did. In return, the employees agreed not to sue the company for work-related injuries. It was "no fault."

The concept proved so popular that by 1920 it had spread to approximately 40 states. This premise of paying the medical bills of injured workers has never been abandoned, and it has become the prime reason that we must include the workers' comp system in our study of health care. Here's why: Because the employer pays all of the medical bills when an employee is hurt on the job, there are no deductibles as there are under traditional medical indemnity programs. It is what the health industry calls "first-dollar" coverage — the employee's bills are covered from the first dollar, not after the patient has spent $50, $100 or more out of pocket in deductibles.

What difference does this make? It makes a huge difference in two ways. First, consider why insurance companies have deductibles: To discourage frivolous visits to the doctor. There is no such restraint in the workers' comp system. Second, and more significantly, it makes a difference because of the way many providers set their fees.

Suppose you're a doctor and your patients are all in a traditional health insurance plan that covers 80 percent of the bill. In other words, for every

$100 charge, the insurance company pays $80 and the patient pays $20. Over time, providers learn that it's difficult sometimes — perhaps most of the time — to collect on that $20 owed by the patient. The provider generally writes that $20 off, but also, they eventually adjust fees to cover the loss.

What happens in reality is that most of the time the provider submits a bill of $120 for a procedure that actually costs $100. Of this $120, the insurance company will pay $96 and the patient owes $24. As before, the provider probably may never see that $24, but with the insurance company now paying $96, essentially full payment is received. Now, what happens when a workers' comp patient comes through the door. This patient isn't going to have to pay a deductible. So the physician is going to bill $120 and is going to get paid $120. The doctor gets "first dollar" treatment just like the patient.

This is a simplification, but you get the point. Multiply this extra $24 by the millions of workers' comp claims every year and the net impact on our national medical bill becomes obvious. We pay that bill, in the form of ever higher premiums, higher deductibles and worst of all, dropped coverage.

But it's not just the lack of deductibles that makes workers' comp so much more expensive. There are other factors at work.

Because of their very nature, workers' comp cases do not have the restraints that insurance companies typically use to control costs. Specifically, in workers' comp cases there are no eliminations for preexisting conditions. Moreover, it is usually the doctor's call alone to decide when the patient is better. So if the injury is to a lower back for instance, it is the doctor who will decide when the patient can return to work.

Of course, most providers in this country still treat lower back injuries subjectively because they refuse to adopt any means of objectively knowing when their patient is better. And some providers, as we have noted, do not want objectivity, lest it threaten their income by allowing patients to exit the system sooner or evaluate the provider's performance. In addition there are always those patients who have determined that it's better to sit home and get paid for watching Oprah than getting paid for going to work.

Why don't insurance companies and employers try to restrain medical spending in workers' comp cases? They do try, but there are limitations. It goes back in part to the deal the employers struck with their employees when the workers' comp system was adopted. The employers agreed to pay their employees' medical bills in return for not being sued, and any cost-cutting measures such as requiring second opinions before allowing a given procedure are not as freely available.

Moreover, the workers' comp requirements are products of state law and as such, the flexibility in the system is dramatically reduced and extremely varied from state to state. A company with locations in 10 states has 10 different sets of bureaucratic regulations to contend with.

So providers treating workers' comp cases are for the most part free to practice as they wish. It's the last vestige of the unrestricted good old days.

What's the result of this unbridled method for treating workplace injuries?

The statistics tell the story: In 1980, the average cost of a workers' comp medical claim was $1,748. In just four years this doubled to $3,564 in 1984, and it nearly doubled again by 1990 to $6,611. The premiums paid by employers for their workers' comp mirror this trend. In 1980, employers paid a total of $22.3 billion in workers' comp premiums. By 1991, this had ballooned to $62 billion.

A study by the Minnesota Department of Labor and Industry supplies more pointed evidence. The study compared the costs for treating injuries through the workers' comp system and through regular indemnity (health) insurance. It found that back injuries cost an average of $308 in medical bills and took an average of 21 days to treat when financed through the workers' comp system. But, back injuries treated through the indemnity system only cost an average of $132 and took an average of just 10 days to treat.

For sprains and strains, $167 and eight days through workers' comp, versus $84 and 1 day through indemnity. Lacerations, $127 through workers' comp, versus $87 through indemnity (both required one day of treatment), and for lower limb fractures, $287 through workers' comp versus $220 through indemnity.

But wait. It gets worse.

We have noted that the premise of workers'
comp is that the workers agree not to sue their
bosses in return for having their medical expenses
covered when they are injured on the job. Well,
that's the way it USED to be. Not anymore. In the
past few decades the courts have chipped away at
this principle. Now, the workers' comp system has
been so convoluted that it is a one-way street. The
workers can now sue their employers for additional items like stress, and for punitive damages, but
the employer still has to pay the medical bills. This
too has had disastrous consequences for our national health costs.

Put yourself in the position of a judge at a
workplace injury trial. The lawyers for the injured
worker are asking for punitive damages and compensation for the worker's stress. Well, how do
you decide how much compensation the worker is
entitled to for the stress? What yardstick do you
use? Most likely you gauge how much the worker
suffered by one simple measure: How much were
the medical bills? If the medical bills are huge,
there must have been a lot of stress involved and
the disability must be permanent or at least serious
and long term — right?

The results are predictable. Physicians treating workplace injuries are urged, by the worker's
attorney, to jack the medical bill as high as possible
in order to fortify their case in court — all under the
guise of making sure that the injured worker is
given the very best of care. No Rolls Royce is good
enough for the injured worker. And remember,
there is very little restraint to impede health care

providers from cooperating with the lawyers. They are getting paid for each procedure. And no second opinions or deductibles are required.

Finally, consider that the injured worker usually has plenty of incentive to go along with a prolonged and expensive treatment. That's because, thanks to workers' comp reform passed in 1972 under President Nixon, many workers actually are better off financially being disabled. This reform act was intended to address the hardship to injured workers because benefits had not kept up with inflation. A presidential commission recommended a sharp increase in benefits, and most states adopted a standard of paying employees 80 percent of their net pay — tax free.

Put it all together and you have a win-win-win situation, as long as you are the provider, the worker or the lawyer. But there is a big loser, of course, and that's the rest of us paying the bill for all this winning.

THE WORKERS' COMP MAZE

Faced with soaring premiums for health insurance, many companies switched to self-insurance during the late 1980's and early 1990's. They found that paying health costs out-of-pocket was actually cheaper than being part of an insurance pool.

Now, companies are facing the same problem of soaring costs with their workers' comp premiums. But they're finding it much harder to restore market discipline by fleeing the insurance companies. Why? Because of the maze of regulations that control workers' comp.

Unlike health insurance, which is a negotiable benefit, workers' comp is a legal requirement, and before any company can self-insure, it has to prove that it has the financial stability to pay claims. This means submitting its books to state regulators and then, in most cases, posting a bond, letter of credit or some other security to guarantee claims.

And the requirements can vary so much from one state to the next that they have been described as "Byzantine." If a company's business crosses state lines, as is common these days, it must meet the requirements of each state where it has employees. This is another significant difference from traditional health insurance. Federal law exempts self-insured health plans from state regulations, so one health plan can serve all the employees of a self-insured company, no matter how many states it covers. There is no such exemption for workers' comp. For employers it is a bureaucratic labyrinth.

Section 3:

How Do We Get Out?

SO WHAT ARE THE FACTS?

a. What was the cost to employers for workers' compensation insurance premiums in each of the following years?
1960?
1970?
1980?
1990?
2000?

Answers:
a. 1960 $2.1   Billion
    1970 $4.9   Billion
    1980 $22.3 Billion
    1990 $56.0 Billion
    2000 $150.0 Billion (est.)

CHAPTER 11:
IDENTIFY THE
REAL CULPRIT

In the 1970's a movement arose in the legal community to develop and market a new product called pre-paid legal insurance. The concept was straight-forward and seemingly benign: To guarantee that no one would go without legal services, the policy holder would simply pre-pay a monthly amount. (Sound similar to Blue Cross in 1932?) To meet this noble goal, the lawyers proposed adapting a health-insurance type system to the law. Just like health insurance, people would pay monthly premiums and in return have access to a lawyer whenever they needed one.

There was as usual more to it than an altruistic motive. Simply put, someone had analyzed how our health system works — I mean, really works — and how, through the rise of the third party payer system, doctors had created a lucrative financial structure for health care that insulated them from having to look the patient in the eye and discuss how much something cost. If it worked so beautifully for doctors, it could work as well for lawyers.

Fortunately for America, the market wanted no part of this scheme and the idea eventually died, albeit with a good deal of pious posturing by the legal community about the injustice that would be perpetrated on Americans too poor to afford regular legal representation to enter into litigation.

The demise of pre-paid legal insurance, before it even started, was fortunate for America because we already are the world's most litigious society. Given the backlog of lawsuits for every imaginable reason, one can only wonder how much more cluttered our courthouses would be if the lawyers had succeeded with this concept.

Think of it: Apply the skyrocketing growth in health care costs, the unnecessary procedures under the rubric of defensive medicine or just plain fraud, and imagine what our legal system would be like if lawyers had been allowed to get away with creating the same unfettered mechanism for their profession.

Imagine the cost to society if we had combined pre-paid legal coverage with our existing contingency fee structure! The system could bankrupt society in a matter of months!

To their credit, the physicians of America did not consciously set out to create our present health care system. Our health care system evolved over the years by happenstance, a labor ruling here, a government program there, and when all the pieces came together they mutated into a cancer on our free-enterprise system.

It is this mutation, this system that has crippled free-market forces, that is the real culprit in what ails American health care. Any reform we undertake will not succeed if we do not identify it for what it is.

As is apparent when we know the facts, it is a mutation in which:

Medical providers, chiefly physicians, controlled the demand for about $700 billion in services in 1992. (That's 80 percent of the $850 billion we spent for health care in 1992.)

Medical providers have financial incentives to perform as many procedures as possible to the patient.

Medical providers can perform many of their services in facilities that they own themselves.

Medical providers are reimbursed for the cost of obtaining equipment that makes them more efficient without any attendant reduction of fees.

Medical providers are reimbursed for the cost of using their equipment. They also receive a tax benefit for owning that equipment, and all of this is **on top of** their usual fees for services.

Medical providers can send the charges to someone other than the patient, which insulates them from confronting the person paying the bill.

The one who ultimately pays the bill, the patient's employer or the government, has dual responsibility for the indemnity (general health) as well as the workers' compensation (industrial accident) portion of the cost as well as extended liability for stress and punitive damages in a supposedly "no fault" legal environment. Put all these features together and we have the same system I described in the restaurant. We have a system structured so that when everyone acts rationally (that is, in their own best economic interest), costs inevitably spin out of control.

Doctors may be somewhat innocent of creating this monstrous system, something that the lawyers who tried to start legal insurance can not claim. But, as the beneficiaries of this system, doctors certainly know where their interests now lie. The last thing the AMA wants is any reform that would end the lucrative system of magic pockets that has brought them as a group wealth that very few Americans will ever realize—and all that with almost no economic risk.

When was the last time you heard of a doctor or medical p.a. (professional association) declaring bankruptcy? An employer based, third party payer system is the single biggest flaw in our health care system because, as I have explained, it insulates patients from the true cost of medicine. It neutralizes the checks and balances of the marketplace. Because the patients, the people receiving the service, are not the ones who pay the bill, patients have no incentive to see that they get their money's worth. They have no incentive to question whether the obstetrician really needs to do three ultrasounds, at $175 each, during the course of a routine pregnancy.

This doesn't happen when you buy a car or any other product or service. Certainly, the salesman will try to talk you into the upgraded stereo system and the die-cast aluminum wheels. But he's got to sell you on it. You're going to be paying for them.

If they cost more than you want to pay, you will have a lot of incentive to turn him down. If he's a good enough salesman you may end up with the upgraded stereo and the die-cast aluminum wheels even though you didn't want them. But that's your fault, not the system's.

If cars were sold like health care is in the United States, when the salesman suggested the upgraded stereo you'd make sure that it also included a CD player, and when he asked about the aluminum wheels, you'd probably ask if white-walls were available, too. And you would do this without a second thought. After all, you'd be entitled to the best, right? And why worry about the cost, you're not paying the bill.

So our first order of business, if we are to have true health reform, must be to overcome this fundamental weakness. There are other changes which need to be made, but first we must correct the skewed incentives, which begin with an employer based, third-party payer system that has health care on auto pilot for escalating costs.

Obviously, health care is so expensive that we cannot totally abandon our health insurance system. We cannot return to a pure free-market process where everyone pays for medical care out of pocket (or with pigs and tomatoes). Few of us have pockets sufficiently deep for that solution.

Nor am I saying that we have to dismantle our current health care system and build a new one from scratch, or replace it with a system copied from another country, such as Canada. We don't need a radically different organization.

We do need a radically different way of handling the incentives that support this system. If we can level the tilted incentives that have led to the disastrous consequences of the past 30 years, we will not need to abandon the present health care system because it will correct itself. The first objective is to create incentives for doctors to act prudently and provide high quality/low cost service. The second objective is to restore the watchdog role of the consumers — empower them with the right to make informed choices about treatment — without relinquishing the concept of universal health insurance.

On the face of it, these would appear to be contradictory goals. In the coming chapters, we will explore ways in which we can accomplish both.

The first step is to blow away the smoke screens that have been thrown up to protect a very lucrative system.

HOW NOT TO BUILD
A HEALTH INSURANCE SYSTEM

*(An excerpt from a CFO magazine commentary
by Uwe Reinhardt)*

Imagine the following scenario: You and a group of equally well-educated and well-meaning colleagues are invited to a dinner at which the spirits flow like water. Eventually all of you are too impaired to drive home (this is imaginary, remember). Instead you play a game called "Building a health insurance system." Would anyone, even in the most drunken stupor, construct a system that: ties the health-insurance coverage of an entire family to one particular job in one particular company, in a way that causes that family to lose that coverage should that job be lost; leads employees to hold on to jobs they loathe, merely to have health insurance; tells families without employer-provided health insurance that their premiums will be sky-high should one or several members of the family be stricken with chronic illness; sometimes simply denies any health insurance coverage to families or small businesses with chronically ill members; tells a family, stricken with illness and without insurance, that it must pauperize itself before society will stretch out a helping hand in the form of Medicaid; has members of uninsured families die at a much higher rate from given illnesses than do similarly situated families that do have insurance coverage; allows the private insurance carriers that cover individuals or small businesses to eat up over a third of the premiums they collect in the form of commissions, administrative overhead and profits; saddles doctors, hospitals, patients, and companies with a claims process whose sheer waste of paper and time is unmatched anywhere else in the world; has the executives of even the largest corporations humble themselves in testimony before lawmakers with their lament that they simply cannot control the cost of providing their employees with health insurance, and that they therefore can no longer compete effectively in the international marketplace? If you were a misanthrope with a truly wicked streak, you might dream up such a scheme, drunk or not. What is truly sobering is that the system I have just described is, of course, the U.S. health insurance system.

SO WHAT ARE THE FACTS?

a. In 1979, how much was spent per capita for health care in the U.S.?

b. In 1990, how much was spent per capita for health care in the U.S.?

c. In 1991, how much was spent per capita for health care in the U.S.?

d. Out of every dollar spent on health care, how much goes for administrative costs?

Answers:
a. $900
b. $2,566
c. $3,160
d. 25%

CHAPTER 12:
GET THE COSTS ON
THE TABLE

The next time you have a doctor's appointment, look your doctor square in the eye and ask what the charge will be. If yours is like most doctors, you'll probably hear either, "I don't know, my office manager takes care of that." or, "Don't worry about it. Your insurance will cover it."

Rare is the doctor who will look you back in the eye and answer you straight out. Why is this? A lot of it has to do with how physicians view themselves and their profession. Physicians invariably think of themselves as healers, as people who cure the sick and comfort the disabled. It's a noble calling, a profession, an avocation. It's not a job. And hence, in their view, it is unseemly to tarnish their image by getting too close to something as tawdry as discussing money. Another reason is they genuinely don't know — it's the business manager's job to worry about such details.

Luckily for them, our insurance system has evolved in such a way that few doctors ever need to discuss fees. Consider what happens when a patient enters a waiting room to be "admitted into

the practice" — to establish a contract with a health
care provider. After name, date of birth, and social
security number, the very first question — well
before vital statistics and personal health and medical history, even before the immediate conditions
that brought the patient to this particular waiting
room — is "what insurance will pay the bill?"

So we don't ask how much it costs and the
doctor doesn't have to say. That's a matter established between the doctor and the insurance company.

"But wait," you say. "We're not talking about
a new car or a stereo. We're talking about our
health, and the skills of those who deliver our
health care may be just as important as price. So it's
naive to think of comparing doctors on the basis of
fees alone."

Congratulations! You've just injected the emotional component about health care that muddles
clear thinking and makes it so hard to be rational
about reforming the system. Yes, health care is a
matter of relieving discomfort and of life and death,
and in this it claims a unique status. But our
purpose here is to help get past these emotional
hang-ups: Just because health care can be literally
a matter of life or death, why should we stick with
a health care system that is life or death to our
society as a whole?

Let's consider a similar case where skills have
as much to do as price with customer satisfaction.
Let's consider the car repair business. Like doctors, good auto mechanics can build a loyal following of customers who come to them without think-

ing twice about the charge. And yet we seem to have competition among auto mechanics. Certainly, the cost of auto repairs has not been rising, like medicine, at two or three times the rate of inflation. Why is this?

Think about how most of these auto mechanics got their customers. In most cases, they didn't inherit them. They did not buy out somebody else's "automobile mechanics practice." Oh, they get some customers by word of mouth, but they earned most of their customers by giving a reasonable estimate and performing adequate services. At one time, these customers were new to the marketplace and were shopping for a mechanic. Odds are they had a specific problem, say, worn brakes, and they shopped for a place to repair them. And the odds are, as they shopped around, they asked the first most basic question of the free market system, "What do you charge for a brake job?" And then maybe another fundamental question, "When can you actually perform this service?" And perhaps finally a third basic question, "What guarantee or warranty will I have on the goods and services provided?" (Imagine asking a doctor if he will refund all or even a part of the costs if a procedure is unsuccessful — even more, imagine asking the doctor if he or she will compensate you in some way if procedures actually worsen your condition!)

It is the basic market pressure, the need to compete for new customers, that keeps auto-repair prices in line. It is the failure — the almost literal inability in our health care system — to ask the same kinds of questions of our doctors that we routinely ask of auto mechanics and other providers of services in the free market place that makes health care cost so great a threat to our national economy.

Certainly, once the mechanic has attracted a customer, his competence will decide whether the customer stays with him. Like physicians, we want an auto mechanic we can have faith in: One who will be competent and will not gouge the customer by saying that things need repairing that really don't. And once a mechanic has won our trust we may well stay with him even if another mechanic offers lower prices.

Regardless, the pertinent fact is that at some point, our mechanic had to earn our patronage, and both price and quality are part of the equation. In medicine, they rarely are.

Costs alone are not the only problem. We also need to address the issue of cost versus competence. In some procedures, competence truly does take on life or death importance, such as in open-heart surgery. And in these cases, it is better to pay more to assure quality. The best proof of this can be found in insurance companies' (and recently the federal government's) preference to fly customers to distant cities in order to use specialists known to excel in their field.

That's why corporations in Cleveland, Ohio, which have formed their own insurance company for health care, began flying patients to the Mayo Clinic, in Minnesota, rather than use local hospitals for complicated procedures. (And under the

Federal Employees system, re-dos at Mayo for poor performance are free.)

Insurance companies don't fly their customers all over the country out of an altruistic belief that their customers deserve the best care available in the country. They do it because it makes financial sense. They have learned from experience that it's cheaper in the long run. The patient heals faster, has a better recovery and suffers fewer complications. Compare the cost of the airfare with the cost of two extra weeks in the intensive care unit because of complications and it's clear which option costs less.

Competence, in these complicated cases, is actually cheaper in the long run. But, is has to be emphasized that this situation is the exception to the rule. For the vast majority of medical procedures, it makes little difference who delivers the care. Routine preventive care and even minor procedures can be given by any competent provider, including nurse practitioners, just as any competent mechanic ought to be able to tune your engine or change your brakes.

And there is no reason why, for this level of care, doctors should not compete on the basis of price. Doctors, aware of the black eye they have given themselves, have belatedly agreed that they ought at least appear to have their customers' interests at heart. So at its annual convention in 1992, the AMA voted that doctors should post their fee schedules.

The policy, of course, is not binding. And fee schedules are hardly a prominent feature of hospital waiting rooms, private doctors offices, and walk-in clinics. It is a lamentable commentary on the sacrosanct position of the medical profession in our society that our states, counties, and municipalities routinely require taxi drivers and "innkeepers" to post their rates prominently and auto mechanics to furnish estimates but require no such disclosure by doctors.

Part of the additional fallout that we now have to endure in the present system is that because consumers don't shop around, insurance companies shop around for them. That's what the insurance companies essentially are doing when they require you to get a second opinion or have a procedure pre-cleared. It goes like this: Your doctor says you should have your gall bladder out. Before he can operate, however, your insurance company insists that you get a second opinion. Or maybe it gives you a form for the doctor to fill out, detailing what his charges are going to be. You have to mail in the estimate to the insurance company. The insurance company will then scrutinize the charge for reasonableness before agreeing to cover the bill. Maybe it will write you back, saying that it will cover only so much of the bill and the rest is up to you if you choose to have the procedure. Before your doctor can put you in the hospital, he or she has to call your insurance company and get its approval. The doctor may say he expects you to be in the hospital for three days. The insurance company will say he's cleared to admit you for two days and to call again if the third day is necessary.

Your doctor puts up with the inconvenience of all this because the market forces him to. (The market, in this case, being the insurance companies which control the purse strings.)

Now, this process may attempt to save money, but most scholars of our health care system question whether getting a second opinion does usually save money. Members of the medical fraternity are loath to offend other colleagues or impinge on their established right to perform whatever services they see fit. But we all pay, in the form of higher administrative costs required because the insurance companies have to do something that customers do for themselves in virtually all other segments of the market. We pay for a whole layer of policing because the creator of demand (the provider) and the customer (the patient) have no training or motivation to be efficient in quality and price. Remember, the current mentality is, "More Is Better!"

PHYSICIAN GREED PLAGUES HEALTH CARE

(An excerpt taken from Business Insurance, *July 22, 1991)*

To the editor: Joanne Wojcik's story in your May 20 issue on the Grumbach-Lee Report, "How many physicians can we afford?" ... helps to focus attention on perhaps the most critical element of the current health care cost crisis: There are too many doctors chasing — and catching — excessively high incomes.

I have yet to find, however, that any of the many recent studies, reports, papers and analyses has come right out and made this very logical, but perhaps difficult to swallow, observation. Average and median physician incomes increased significantly during the 80's, both in absolute terms and more importantly, relative to the average income of all wage earners. Hence, practitioners of an occupation already enjoying one of the highest standards of living in history made gains at the expense of society as a whole, while working fewer hours (this is also well documented) and all this while a material segment of society did not have access to their services.

If the crisis in health care financing is to have any real chance of being eased, this "favored profession" status of physicians must change. If a solution is going to be fair, someone is going to have to give up something, and it is clear that physicians, whose incomes are certainly one of the primary causes of the crisis, have the most to give.

As physicians' income per unit of work has skyrocketed, studies have found that many of their services are unnecessary, inefficient and in some cases, actually more harmful than helpful to patient health. This waste has made it more frustrating because of the political power of physicians and their various organizations. Efforts to implement lower cost procedures and to utilize lower cost personnel (nurse practitioners, for example) are constantly impeded by the iron-fisted control of those who determine what constitutes the practice of medicine.

If controls on physician incomes cause some doctors to stop practicing medicine in protest of outside influences on their business, it would perhaps be in the country's best interest. It would also suggest that the dollar has provided more incentive for persons to practice medicine than the humanitarian motives so often cited.

I suspect that one of the greatest cancers endangering the health of our health care system is that of greed. Physicians, it is time to heal yourselves.

Hobson D. Carroll
President,
Employee Benefit Specialists Inc.
Minneapolis.

147

SO WHAT ARE THE FACTS?

a. In 1989, how many Medicare enrollees were there?

b. In 1989, how much did Medicare pay out?

c. In the State of California in 1992, what percent of the stress in your life had to be job-related to qualify for disability payments?

d. Between 1980 and 1992 what percent increase in stress claims occurred in the State of California?

Answers:
a. 33.6 Million
b. $94 Billion
c. 10%
d. 700%

CHAPTER 13:
EDUCATE THE
PATIENT

Let's revisit our orthopedic surgeon who was practicing on the cadaver's leg on the eve of doing his first knee replacement. But this time, let's approach it from the patient's perspective. Do you think for a minute that this patient knew that he was the first person on whom this doctor was performing this procedure? Didn't he go to a specialist in order to make sure that the person who was cutting on him knew what he was doing?

We don't know what happened to this unsuspecting patient. It may be that the surgery went fine and there were no adverse effects. Or maybe the surgery seemed fine at first but within six months the patient needed another operation to fix what was done wrong the first time. (In most cases re-dos aren't free!)

Either scenario is beside the point. The point is that this patient was not an informed medical consumer. On the contrary! He was by implication misinformed by being led to believe that he was in the hands of a surgical specialist well-versed and experienced in all procedures undertaken by him.

Had he been properly informed about this surgeon's experience, it is doubtful that he would have put himself in the position of being on the lower end of this surgeon's learning curve. Then again, maybe he would have allowed the surgeon to proceed, but only after negotiating a reduced fee to account for the surgeon's lack of experience in this procedure or possibly free follow-up surgery if something went wrong.

Before we can have a medical system that functions effectively, we must make sure that we give patients the tools they need to educate themselves to the realities of cost and quality — the same realities that govern the other buying decisions we make. You can buy the Honda or you can buy the Escort. If the Escort offers all the features of the Honda, and it costs $4,000 less, you may well buy the Escort. On the other hand, the Honda might have a better reputation and track record for quality, and you may decided that it's worth the extra $4,000. Regardless, you are aware of the quality distinctions, you are aware of the cost distinctions, and you weigh the two accordingly before making your choice.

In medicine, you can judge neither quality nor cost, because the information, by design, is simply not available. And rare indeed is the patient who demands such information even if doctors were willing to make it available. Culturally, we've grown accustomed to the philosophy that the doctor knows best. We trust our doctors to be competent at what they do and to have our best interest, not their bottom line, at heart. So when they recommend a procedure, we tend to take his word for it. But wouldn't it be more reasonable if we could look our doctor in the eye and ask, "Before I agree to this, where are the studies that verify its effectiveness?" or "Can you give me some references of patients on whom you have done this procedure?" Or wouldn't it make sense to be able to ask about other physicians who have undergone the procedure in question?

One telling way to judge a procedure is to see how many doctors submit to the procedure themselves. For example, in the field of lower back pain, you will find that doctors practically never have back surgery themselves. The reason is simple. They know that it usually doesn't work. This, however, has not stopped legions of back specialists from recommending back surgery, such as discectomys (removal of disc tissue from between the vertebra), when 88 percent of all back disorders are muscular in origin.

Unfortunately, if you question doctors, or ask about quality, experience, or cost, they will probably allude to the essential trust necessary between doctor and patient and subtly suggest that you should go elsewhere. Good advice! Although it was probably not what you thought you wanted to hear. If a doctor can't stand a little well-intentioned, informed heat, it is probably time to get out his kitchen.

Recently, a new wave of consumer awareness has sprung up to help medical consumers make better choices. This movement is rooted in an institution with the unwieldy name of The Foundation for Informed Medical Decision Making. That's a mouthful, but it sums up the foundation's mission: To help patients make better decisions about their health care.

As its starting point, The Foundation challenges the AMA's bedrock premise that only doctors have the knowledge and the clinical experience to make judgment calls such as whether to have a certain operation.

The Foundation was started by doctors and medical researchers at Dartmouth University who noticed an incredible variance in the rate of prostate surgery in two Maine counties next to each other. In one county, 55 percent of the men with prostate trouble had surgery. In the other, only 15 percent of the men with this condition had surgery.

Upon investigating, the researchers found that in the first county, the prevailing medical opinion, shared throughout the local medical community as the acceptable standard of treatment, was that early prostate surgery was necessary. In the other, doctors believed that surgery should be only a last resort. (This variance shows vividly the need to develop standard medical practice patterns due to the wide variations from one community to the next.) Yet, the ultimate conclusion was that the health of prostate patients in both counties was roughly the same. Obviously much more money, time, pain, and suffering were expended in the county with the high surgical rate. Yet, the outcomes were identical.

From this study, the researchers concluded that patients need to get involved in making medical decisions; The Foundation was created to do just that. The Foundation accomplishes its task by using interactive videos that present all aspects of a given procedure. Because their study in Maine gave them a data base, they began with prostate surgery. They produced a video that presented a complete look at the operation, the good it can do, and the adverse consequences that can result. Most importantly, it included interviews with men who have had the surgery; some who were pleased and others who were displeased with the results.

The video had dramatic results. In a pilot project involving 250 men in Denver, the rate of surgery fell 44 percent. In a follow-up study in Seattle, surgery rates fell 60 percent. Predictably, some doctors don't like this approach because they say it undermines their clinical judgment.

It is impossible to know how much their objections also are rooted in the loss of income. But it seems to be a factor. Doctors in HMO's, which receive a set fee per patient, have been much more receptive to the video than doctors who charge by the service. A group practice in Iowa, where doctors work under the traditional fee-for-service arrangement, received the video but few patients were urged to watch it. To combat this, insurance companies have actually even considered paying the fee-for-service doctors to show the video!

The Foundation now has subsequently produced videos for mild hypertension, breast cancer surgery, breast cancer therapy, and low back pain. Videos for labile angina, prostate screening, and prostate treatment are scheduled for future release. For all of them, the guiding principle is the same, as Dr. John Wennberg, one of the founders, said in 1991: "Patients need to know that they have choices and that having surgery is not like getting your hair cut." As we've said, it is not enough just to give patients the ability to judge quality.

They also have to balance quality with cost. Getting doctors to post their fees and discuss them would be a big step in the right direction. But patients also need to know that medical fees are arbitrary.

Tom Wright, the owner of a company that makes labels for the furniture industry, learned this when his wife had surgery on her sinuses. Before the surgery, the doctor estimated that the surgery would cost $5,800. But when the bill arrived, it was $7,700. Wright, understandably perturbed, wrote the doctor, and without making any accusations, asked for an explanation. The doctor wrote back that his billing computer had charged separately (i.e., unbundled) for three procedures that were performed, even though there was only one incision, and that the $5,800 was the right charge. He added that the $5,800 is what he would send to the insurance company knowing he might not get full reimbursement, and that he'd be happy to take 80 percent of that charge. So Wright owed the doctor $4,700. The original bill was $7,700, but the doctor accepted $4,700.

Wright has seen other questionable billing practices. He's found doctors who were willing to artificially inflate their bill so that the patient would not have to make his copayment.

Why is Tom Wright a careful medical consumer? It's because he, in fact, is also the medical payer. As the owner of his own company, Wright is the one paying the insurance premiums for these health benefits, and he knows that his premiums are directly tied to the how much his employees use the system. He is the man who pays the bill, so he is the one watching the costs.

If our medical system were set up so that everybody watched costs just as carefully, it is plausible to imagine that medical costs would not be going up at twice the rate of inflation, but actually going down.

Currently the system is not geared that way. Even if you want to keep track of your own medical costs, it can be quite a challenge. That's because medical spending is so fractured. Your employer may pay part of the premium. And you may pay part. Then there may be copayments per visit and per procedure, or annual deductibles, or certain procedures that are not covered at all.

In such a system, it takes a concerted effort to keep track of your actual medical spending. It is difficult even when there are no mistakes, delays, or confusing seemingly contradictory account statements — which is almost never the case in billing systems notorious for their unparalleled complexity and errors.

Any medical reform, if it is to control costs by using market forces, must allow the patients to know just how much the care costs them both directly and indirectly through costs paid by others and ultimately passed on to them.

BUNDLING WARS

If you were a tailor making a pair of trousers, you would be only too happy to be able to charge separately for putting in the zipper, for the pockets, for the belt loops, even for each stitch.Tailors don't get to charge separately for each small part of their work. But doctors do. It's called unbundling. That's why, when a father in North Carolina took his son to the emergency room to have a cut stitched up, the doctor didn't bill him one fee for closing the wound. The doctor billed him, literally, by the stitch: $105 each; $525 for five stitches that probably took less than two minutes each to put in. I know this because the father works for me.

How do doctors learn to do this? Any doctor worth his country club membership knows about St. Anthony Publishing. Armed with the advice in its helpful newsletters, providers can stay one step ahead of the insurance companies in the cat-and-mouse game of billing for maximum income.

For example, one issue of **St. Anthony's Coding for OB/ GYN Reimbursement Newsletter** *explained how to unbundle fees for dilatation and curettage. By billing separate charges for dilatation, for curettage, and even for sterile dressings, one practice increased its average fee from $300 to $538, and the practice increased its gross revenue by 78 percent.*

Another newsletter explained the financial advantages of "superbilling," that is, issuing patients detailed bills that split hairs over the procedures they perform. By doing this, family practitioners could increase their weekly revenue up to $845, or $40,500 a year, the newsletter promised. St. Anthony's is part of an entire industry selling books, newsletters (at last count there were 11), and seminars to teach providers how to exploit the system by coding Medicare and insurance bills for maximum income. For example, the brief discharge visits should be coded as a "medical conference" because some insurance companies don't pay when the bill is coded for "hospital discharge day management."

This, inevitably, has led the insurance companies to take counter measures. Some have invested in computer programs to "rebundle" bills. For example, appendix operations coded for both appendectomy and for laparotomy (the abdominal incision) are refigured for just the appendectomy. The bill for the incision is thrown out, since a doctor has to make an incision anyway to perform an appendectomy. This saves $1,000.

SO WHAT ARE THE FACTS?

a. How much of the cost of each car produced by the top three American auto manufacturers in 1992 represented the cost of health care for automobile workers?

b. What percent of patients who enter hospitals contract additional diseases?

c. In 1972, how many practicing physicians were there per 100,000 population?

d. In 1992, how many practicing physicians were there per 100,000 population?

Answers:

a. $600 at Ford
   $900 at GM
   $1,100 at Chrysler

b. 8%

c. 153

d. 220

CHAPTER 14:
REALLOCATE THE TAX
BENEFITS

Consider the case of two men who work in the same city, have similar family situations, have similar health insurance plans, and make roughly the same amount of money. One man is an accounting consultant and has incorporated his business. He buys his own health insurance for $4,500 a year. The other works for a small advertising firm that does not offer health insurance, and he too buys his own health insurance for $4,500.

All things considered, the men are in roughly the same financial boat, but one man, the consultant, fares far better at tax time because he gets to deduct every penny he spends on health insurance from his taxes. The advertising executive only gets to deduct part of it — if he doesn't make too much money. If, in fact, the advertising person's health premiums are less than a certain percentage of his adjusted gross income, he gets to deduct nothing.

Why? Think back to Chapter 8 when I discussed the rise of organized labor. In 1948, the IRS ruled that corporations could deduct the cost of providing health insurance for their employees. It was one way the government lessened the burden on business in the wake of ruling that health benefits were legitimate grounds for a strike. In case one, the accountant gets to deduct $4,500 from his taxable income. This may save him as much as $1,800 in taxes, leaving a net cost of $2,700 for his insurance. In case two, the advertiser gets no tax benefit and in essence is paying for health care with $4,500 after-tax dollars. To put it another way, the advertising man has to earn about $7,000 to net after-tax the $4,500 used to pay for his health care. Thus the real price difference after taxes between the advertiser ($7,000) and the accountant ($2,700) is $4,300. ($7,000 minus $2,700 = $4,300) This inherent injustice of the system is wrong.

But a far graver consequence is that we have become a nation that provides health care through the workplace. And now, in this era of soaring health costs, this system is failing our society as more and more people find themselves locked into jobs lest they lose their insurance if they relocate. This inability to continue coverage is contributing to the number of people who do not have insurance at all. Two-thirds of the 37 million people who do not have health insurance in this country are workers or their dependents. Perhaps some of them could afford insurance if they got the same tax break that employers get. (In truth, however, this 37 million uninsured is a revolving number. About 27 million of the 37 million have no insurance for about 4 months during which time they are between jobs or unemployed. The net number of hard core, continuously uninsured persons in this country is about 10 million.) Given the current mess, it's time to change the tax laws to reallocate the tax benefits to meet today's needs and to bring market forces to bear on health costs.

How would such a revamped system work? Imagine that the tax laws have been changed and every taxpayer can deduct all of his or her health costs. Imagine that employers no longer provide health insurance, but they do give employees an annual bonus or some other compensation that is equal to what the company would have spent for their employees' health insurance. The employees then shop for health insurance and pay their premiums with the increased income.

What is the net result? For employers it's a wash. The money they once spent on employee health insurance now is paid directly to the employees. Employers can deduct these payments from their taxes as employee compensation, just as before they deducted what they spent on health insurance.

The employees come out even better. Employees get to choose the health plan that fits their personal life-styles, rather than having to take the plan offered by the boss, and it doesn't cost them any more than before. In fact, the employees potentially have more disposable income because they now get the tax benefit. Those who do not make enough to buy health insurance without gutting the family budget would receive a tax credit instead of a tax deduction (tax credits are deducted from the income tax you owe, tax deductions are deducted from the income on which you have to pay tax). And, if the tax credit were more than the taxes owed, the government would issue a refund check to make up the difference.

Suddenly, we now purchase our own health insurance and we personally have every normal human motivation to keep our costs down. Our health system is better off because now the person who receives the medical service is also paying the bill for the insurance coverage. We're beginning to restore some sanity to the medical marketplace by creating 250 million personal watchdogs for the system — us.

Another concept, proposed by a group of insurance companies banded together as the Council for Affordable Health Insurance, is to create "medical IRA's."

Once again, the idea is to reallocate the way medical dollars flow into the system in order to bring market forces to bear on health costs. Here's how it would work: Employers would split the money they spend on health insurance per employee into two pots, one for the insurance company and one for the employee. The money sent to the insurance company would be used to buy a policy with a rather high deductible. The money given to the employee would be used to pay the deductible.

For example, say the ACME Tool Co. used to spend $4,500 per employee for a comprehensive health plan. With medical IRA's, ACME might switch to a policy with a $2,500 annual deductible and that costs only $2,000 per employee. The other $2,500 that ACME is no longer paying in premiums would instead be put into the employee's medical IRA. The employee would use this money through the course of the year to pay for medical services. When the employee had spent all of his medical IRA for the year, he also would have met his annual deductible, so he would not face any further costs. On the other hand, if the employee did not spend all of his medical IRA in a given year, it would be his to do with as he pleased — either roll it over to the following year or maybe use it to help pay holiday bills.

Once again, under this set-up the person receiving the service would be paying the bills — at least, the first $2,500 of them. And at the same time, the employees would have the very best incentive for holding down costs. So they might decide that they really don't need to pay a specialist $1,000 to remove that blemish when the family doctor says he can do it for $250. And they might decide that they can get just as good an annual physical from the nurse practitioner as they could from an MD, and at one-third the cost.

Under this system, we would be the ones guarding against unnecessary services and scrutinizing bills for overcharges. There would be 250 million watch dogs on the system instead of tens of thousands insurance screeners who bear an administrative burden of about $67 billion annually.

COMPLEXITY "R" US:
AN EXCERPT FROM IRS PUBLICATION 17 ON DEDUCTING HEALTH INSURANCE

If you were self-employed and had a net profit for the year, were a general partner (or a limited partner receiving guaranteed payments) or if you received wages in 1992 from an S corporation in which you were a more than 2 percent shareholder (who is treated as a partner), you may be able to deduct up to 25 percent of the amount paid for health insurance on behalf of yourself, your spouse, and dependents. Do this on line 26 of Form 1040. If you itemize your deductions, include the remaining premiums with all other medical care expenses on Schedule A, subject to the 7.5 percent limit. You cannot take the deduction if you were eligible to participate in any subsidized health plan maintained by your employer or your spouse's employer during any part of 1992. For more information, get Publication 535, Business Expenses. If you qualify to take the deduction, use the following worksheet to figure out how much you can deduct. But, if any of the following applies, do not use the worksheet. Instead, use the worksheet in Publication 535 to figure your deduction. You had more than one source of income subject to self-employment tax. Your 1992 tax year ended on a date other than December 31, 1992. You file Form 2555, Foreign Earned Income, or Form 2555-EZ. If you can file Schedule EIC, Earned Income Credit, you may also be able to claim the health insurance credit on that schedule. If you do claim that credit, do not use the following worksheet. Instead, use the worksheet in Publication 596, Earned Income Credit.

SO WHAT ARE THE FACTS?

a. For every one medical malpractice suit filed in 1969, how many were filed in 1992?

b. In 1992, how much was spent on prescription drugs in the U.S.?

c. In a tort claim award, what percent goes to
Administrative Costs
Defense Costs
Claimant's Attorney
Claimant's Economic Loss
Claimant's Pain and Suffering

d. What is a "capper"?

Answers:

a. 300

b. $59 Billion

c. Administrative Costs 24%
Defense Costs 18%
Claimant's Attorney 15%
Claimant's Economic Loss 22%
Claimant's Pain and Suffering 21%

d. A "capper" trolls the front of the unemployment office delivering fraudulent workers' compensation claimants to lawyers and doctors.

CHAPTER 15:
REFORM THE TORT
SYSTEM

When it comes to doctors' number one beef, the malpractice system, doctors have a partial credibility problem. They say that the malpractice system is not working. But every time they say this they are all too aware that their gripes can be interpreted as wanting to change the system so that they are not held accountable for their actions.

In all fairness, the doctors have a legitimate point. Our malpractice system is not working. And it needs to be fixed. Mind you, malpractice is not as major a contributor to runaway health coasts that the AMA would have you believe. That Great Lie was exposed for what it is in Chapter 2. But $20 billion is $20 billion, and there is no reason that we should saddle our health system with this expense if some timely changes in the tort law would help.

And changes are needed. Our malpractice system is supposed to protect people from poor quality providers and also compensate their victims, but a study of medical injuries and malpractice that a team of Harvard researchers did for New York State in 1989 shows that our system does neither. The study did validate a common complaint of physicians: That too many ill-founded medical malpractice lawsuits are filed. The researchers compared medical files with malpractice claims actually made and found that for every 100 malpractice claims, only 17 showed any evidence of negligence by the doctor.

In 60 percent of the claims, the researchers could not even find evidence of any medical injury, let alone medical malpractice. Despite this, the study found that plaintiffs in medical malpractice claims were collecting money in roughly 50 out of every 100 claims: 1,900 settlements out of 3,800 claims filed. Score one for the doctors. The evidence suggests that many are, in fact, being unfairly held responsible through the court system.

More precisely, it's cheaper for the doctor to settle than fight even if he or she did nothing wrong.

But that's not the entire story.

When the Center For National Health Program Studies projected the Harvard data to the United States at large, the desperate need for alternatives became even clearer. Of the 33.2 million people admitted to hospitals in 1988, the study found that 332,000 (about 1 percent) suffered from real medical malpractice. Of these 332,000 instances of real malpractice, 45,200 of the patients died.

But of the 332,000 real malpractice cases, there were only 5,100 malpractice lawsuits initiated. Score another one for the doctors in that their real mistakes are only being confronted in the courts about 1.5 percent of the time. For all the 33.2 million total hospital admissions, however, there were about 30,000 total legal claims filed (both real and "trumped up" malpractice claims.)

The statistics thus show that doctors have less than a 1/10th of 1 percent chance of being confronted in the courts for any procedure they perform. And when they are confronted legally, about 98 percent of the claims have no malpractice involved; and 60 percent of the claims have no evidence of injury whatsoever. As we saw above, in 50 percent of the claims there is a pay-off to the patient (and the lawyer) bringing a claim. Score a real big one for the lawyers. You have a 50 percent chance of getting money just by bringing the claim, whether or not it's legitimate. It sure is better odds than any lottery or casino I know of.

And if the lawyer takes the case on a contingency basis, as is almost always the situation, you don't even have to come up with your own ante. It's not going to take a great deal of inducement to begin legal action. One frequent suggestion for reforming tort law, is to adopt the "loser pays" system that is used in Great Britain. Under such a system, the party that loses the lawsuit, regardless of who brought it, pays the legal expense for both sides. That's very different from our system in America, where in virtually all cases each side pays its own legal fees. Because of this system, a whole industry has developed in America in which ambulance-chasing lawyers press lawsuits for free and agree to take their compensation out of whatever settlement their client receives.

In England, because the loser is going to get stuck with the fee, the courts are not jammed with lawsuits for every imaginable reason. In America, there is an over-abundance of evidence that frivolous lawsuits are being pressed and valuable court resources are being squandered.

But wait, you say. Isn't the contingency fee system the only means the poor have to getting legal help? Take that away and only the rich could sue.

That, of course, is every trial lawyer's first defense of the contingency fee system. But it doesn't hold water. For one thing, adopting loser pays would not stop lawyers from accepting cases on contingency. If a poor person had a legitimate complaint, he or she would still find representation because quality lawyers would take real cases. But people with frivolous cases would find it hard to bring lawsuits on a contingency basis. And the ambulance chasers would no longer be so apt to press frivolous lawsuits (knowing as they now do, that under today's system the target of the lawsuit generally finds it more advantageous to settle out of court).

With "loser pays," the targets of frivolous actions would have every reason to mount a full-blown defense, knowing that when they prevailed in court, they would not be out a dime. It would not take too many such cases before the flood of frivolous lawsuits, including unfounded malpractice suits, would diminish. With fewer malpractice suits, malpractice premiums would drop and doctors would feel less compelled to practice defensive medicine.

Nowhere is the industry of ambulance chasing for contingency fees more abused than in the area of workers' compensation. As I discussed in Chapter 10, workers' compensation was supposed to be a no-fault insurance system that paid workers for their medical costs and their lost wages when they were injured on the job. It wasn't supposed to be winning the lottery.

But as we have seen, case law over the years has eroded this premise. And now, lawyers are so blatant about trolling for fees that they run advertisements in newspapers and on television encouraging people to cash in through workers' comp. This practice is especially flagrant in California. So flagrant that in 1992 the state enacted a new law that makes it a felony to submit a fraudulent workers' comp claim.

Armed with this law, one insurance company tried to fight fraudulent claims by placing an ad in the *Los Angeles Times* warning about the new law. The company had the ad placed in the medical services section, where the fee-trollers also advertise. The company's efforts were short lived, however. After a few days, the newspaper moved the ad to the legal notices section of the classifieds. The insurance company complained, saying that this was defeating the purpose of the advertisement. But the newspaper asserted that because the ad was not offering medical services, it could not run it there. It is impossible to tell exactly how much pressure the fee-trollers put on the newspaper to move the ad. But their victory was complete when the insurance company yanked the ad rather than run it as a legal notice and waste the money.

At this point, the realistic way to restore rationality to the workers' comp system is to restore it to its original no-fault concept by ridding it of the embellishments of compensation for punitive damages, stress, pain and suffering, and all of the other nebulous losses the system has come to allow.

If we can return to the no-fault principle, we can consider a different option for reducing the number of medical malpractice lawsuits. We could establish a malpractice compensation system under which legitimate victims of malpractice — as determined by a panel of legal and medical experts — would accept a negotiated settlement arrived at in arbitration in exchange for giving up their right to sue. This would protect doctors from frivolous malpractice claims because they would be eliminated in arbitration by the panel of experts. This would not, however, preclude victims from choosing not to enter arbitration and seeking significant reimbursement through the court in cases that warranted it — and remember, with a loser-pay system only cases with serious legal merit would likely be involved.

WANTED: A DOSE OF COMMON SENSE

If ever there was a doctrine that spurred attorneys to even greater efforts, it is the doctrine, accepted by the courts, of joint and several liability. Under this theory, a company only tangentially related to a product can be held totally liable for compensatory awards. This includes distributors and wholesalers — companies that have absolutely nothing to do with manufacturing a product.

And the deeper a company's pockets, the more the theory is invoked. In fact, it is a necessary means of acquiring the huge damage settlements that give the lawyers more income.

Asbestos litigation is instructive: Huge settlements against companies that used to make asbestos, or products containing asbestos, have forced at least 16 major companies into bankruptcy. Under joint and several liability doctrines applicable to asbestos litigation, the surviving producers of products containing asbestos are left to bear the burden for all asbestos related businesses. And as more companies go bankrupt, those remaining will continue to bear all the liability.

In a column for the Wall Street Journal *in July 1992, Glenn Bailey, the chairman of Keene Corp., outlined how workmen's compensation claims of employees who alleged that they had been harmed by exposure to asbestos in the workplace was affecting his company. Keene has been found liable in asbestos litigation because in 1968 it acquired a subsidiary company which made thermal insulation containing 10 percent asbestos. This subsidiary sold about $15 million of the asbestos product through 1972, when it ceased production. This was out of $500 million in total sales for the subsidiary, which was closed in 1975.* **"Not one of the plaintiffs,"** *Bailey wrote,* **"was ever employed by Keene or the company it bought. In fact, most of them worked in naval shipyards during World War II, 25 years before Keene was formed.** *And here's the greatest irony: Most of these plaintiffs are not sick. They're just worried about what might happen in the future."*

This litigation has cost Keene an average of $800,000 A WEEK. The company has paid out $400 million to settle asbestos litigation. Two-thirds of this, about $265 million — three times as much as has gone to workers — has gone to the fee-trolling attorneys.

This may have something to do with why Keene is now a FORMER Fortune 500 company.

SO WHAT ARE THE FACTS?

a. According to an AMA survey, what percent of the population is beginning to lose faith in doctors?

b. How much did the AMA spend in 1991 on an ad campaign to bolster public opinion of physicians?

c. What percent of one-year-olds are immunized against diphtheria and measles in the USA, Canada, Britain, Sweden, and Japan?

Answers:
a. 69%
b. $1.75 Million
c. USA 70%
Canada 85%
Britain 78%
Sweden 97%
Japan 84%

CHAPTER 16:
TELL US
THE TRUTH,
THE WHOLE TRUTH...

Medicine is the only profession in which everyone is assumed, nay, expected, to be perfect. It's part of the unique status we accord doctors. We don't assume perfection in accountants or lawyers. But we do with doctors.

Popular culture has fed this myth, too, through the "Marcus Welby" syndrome, the television shows that present the physician as demi-gods with a scalpel. And doctors have done nothing to discourage this myth.

The truth, of course, is that doctors make mistakes like everyone else. But unlike the rest of us, who have to live with our mistakes, doctors have erected a system that hides their mistakes, and lets them escape accountability in the market place.

Let me show you what I mean: Cord strangulations, causing death during childbirth, have gone the way of the horse and buggy in modern medicine. They just don't and shouldn't happen. Imagine the surprise, then, when an obstetrician in my community lost two babies to cord strangulation within about 6 months. I followed these events with interest. In any event, after the second cord strangulation the doctor packed his bags and left the state. I asked another obstetrician what had happened to the doctor who had disappeared. The answer: "Oh, he was such a good guy and so involved with so many local Medical Society committees; he just couldn't say no to anyone and he had spread himself so thin that he was just overwhelmed. He needed to cut all ties to the community and go practice in another state so he could get a fresh start. "Besides," I was told, "He's so good and so smart that he really belongs in academic medicine." I was too polite to say what I was thinking: Sure, he's so overworked that he has time to maintain a single-digit handicap at the country club. This I knew personally, because we both belonged to the same club. I can't prove it, but my sense is that the local doctors packed his bags and shipped him out. I subsequently learned that he had joined a practice in another state.

IN THEORY, doctors are held accountable by their state licensing boards and medical societies. But these are clubs for those inside the system. They're run by doctors. So is it any surprise that they are reluctant to actually discipline their members?

A study by the Health Research Group of Public Citizen found that state licensing boards issued a total of about 3,000 disciplinary actions in 1991 for all 50 states. This, Public Citizen said, is a pittance compared to the estimated 150,000 to 300,000 Americans who are killed or injured each year because of medical malpractice. The study had another measure that shows how state boards are failing the public.

The disciplinary rate in the Public Citizen study worked out to 3.4 actions for every 1,000 doctors. But a Tufts University study, conducted in 1989, showed that medical malpractice carriers imposed sanctions in the form of refusal to pay claims, higher premiums, or cancellation of coverage at a rate of 13.6 for every 1,000 doctors. In other words, the disciplinary rate of state boards is only a fourth of what it would be if they held doctors as accountable as insurance companies do. Dr. Sidney Wolfe, the director of Public Citizen's Health Group, has pointed out that state licensing boards vary considerably from state to state. In some states, like Georgia, the state board is very active in sniffing out possible malpractice. In other states, they are do-nothings too ready to make excuses for other doctors. Their reluctance to discipline bad doctors is not, however, the only problem with state medical societies.

Ever try to get a state medical society to give you information about a particular doctor? Unless the board is an exception, it will throw up all sorts of obstacles. When it comes to presenting a united front to the public, doctors take second place to no one, and nowhere is this more evident than in the way that medical societies functional as mutual protection associations. Now, if a truly incompetent physician stays in one community or one state for too long, no amount of stonewalling will protect his reputation from the unflattering word-of-mouth that will eventually spread. But for him, the system has another protection: He can move to another state and start with a clean slate. Licensing boards and medical societies are autonomous entities and they don't share information across state lines.

This is astounding.

Insurance companies, HMO's and credit bureaus certainly share very complete sets of national data bases with detailed information about millions of ordinary citizens that is available not only to themselves but to the general public. The incredible self-protective front of the medical fraternity very deliberately has no such network of information. And as long as this is the case, doctors like our incompetent obstetrician will pick up and move to another state without the public being any the wiser. And our medical system will be handicapped because the consumers of medical care will be denied the information they need to judge quality and avoid incompetence and abuse. Is it overly harsh to saddle a provider for a lifetime with one mistake, to not provide the means to make a fresh start that moving to a new state affords?

Not usually. Studies indicate that 80 percent of the malpractice is committed by 20 percent of the providers. In other words, our current system, in most cases, is not protecting a competent doctor who made one mistake long ago. It's protecting repeat offenders who need to find another way to make a living. Besides, there's nothing to preclude medical societies from adopting a mechanism that purges adverse information about a doctor from the record after a given period of time without further incident. Will health reform fail if we do not do this? Of course not. But in the medical market-place, anything that inhibits the consumer from judging quality and cost is a self-imposed handi-cap that all of society will pay for.

THE IAMETER STORY

Peter Farley, a physician and a pioneer of the biotech industry in the United States, has found a new toehold in health care with a company called Iameter Inc. Farley's focus is quite simple: He analyzes the Medicare data of physicians (who control 80 percent of the health costs), then he puts their practice patterns into one of four categories: 1. High Cost/High Quality, 2. Low Cost/Low Quality, 3. High Cost/Low Quality, or 4. Low Cost/High Quality.

Iameter then does two simple things. First it educates the physicians as to which category they fall into, then secondly, it financially motivates them to practice in the fourth category of Low Cost/High Quality.

It's a simplistically brilliant concept. Iameter has been around for almost 10 years, but only recently has the world paid attention. In Cincinnati, four large employers have hired Iameter to rate 14 hospitals that their employees use. Iameter is compiling information on major diagnostic categories and using this information to compare these hospitals for cost, lengths of stay and outcomes. With this information, the companies can then contract directly for health care with the best hospitals.

The potential savings is enormous. Just based on 1991 data, Iameter found large differences, after adjusting for risk, in the charges for such common procedures as balloon angioplasty (rates varied by up to $8,000) and coronary bypasses (which varied up to $7,000). The company calculated that if all employers in Cincinnati had used the most cost-effective hospitals in 1991, they would have saved $120 million of the $600 million they spent that year on health care.

Will the Iameter study make a difference in Cincinnati? The four employers who sponsored the study (Proctor & Gamble, General Electric Aircraft Engines, The Kroger Co., and Cincinnati Bell Telephone) have a total of about 168,000 employees and dependents out of a total in the city of about 370,000.

If they throw their weight around, the rest of the medical community serving the other citizens of Cincinnati will have to follow. Lawrence Frye, the president of Iameter, told *Business Insurance* *that some of the hospitals were skittish about sharing their data with Iameter, but his comment applies equally to all providers:* **"Historically, they've been in a position of control and this is different. This is wresting control back to the people writing the checks."**

SO WHAT ARE THE FACTS?

a. What percent of health problems could be handled at home with self care?

b. What percent of health problems are treated in doctor's offices?

c. What percent of health costs are represented by treatment in the doctors' office?

d. What percent of health problems are treated in hospitals?

e. What percent of health care costs are represented by hospital treatment?

Answers:

a. 50% - 75%

b. 84%

c. 40%

d. 16%

e. 60%

CHAPTER 17:
EMPOWER
THE PATIENT

Imagine a health care system in which all people could buy their own health insurance. They would shop from one company to the next, from HMO's to insurance companies to PPO's (Preferred Provider Organizations, which are networks of doctors organized by insurance companies), comparing facilities, benefits, prices and picking the one that best meets their needs, at prices they could afford.

A bit of utopia?

Not at all. That's how 9 million Americans buy their health insurance. Who are these people? They are the employees and dependents, current and retired, of the federal government. They get their insurance through the Federal Employee Health Benefits system, and they offer proof that free market forces can control health costs if they are given a chance. Since 1959, when the federal system was set up, it has a track record that shows what happens when consumers control the marketplace. Under the system, federal employees have about 400 options for getting their health care, ranging from traditional insurers such as

Blue Cross/Blue Shield, to more than 300 managed-care plans. The costs of these options range from about $350 a year to over $4,000 a year, depending on family status, extent of coverage and other choices the consumer makes.

Generally speaking, the federal government pays about 60 percent of the cost and the employee pays the rest. Because it is up to the employee to pick the health plan, the employee must get involved. The employee is not dictated his health plan, as happens in most companies that provide health insurance. The employee decides. The employee has the motivation to shop carefully and compare benefits.

And in the test that counts — that of how well costs are regulated by the consumer — the federal system passes with flying colors. At a time when most insurance premiums were going up by double-digit percentages, premiums per employee in the federal system went up an average of just 3 percent in 1993. And this is despite all the other baggage that our health system is burdened with — too many specialists, self-referrals, too much technology, excessive administrative costs, etc. This is what happens when we put the patient in control.

Yet most suggestions to switch to a consumer-based system are met with one main major objection: The general public can't be trusted to make the right choice when it comes to medicine — the subject is too complicated for our simple minds. This, as the federal employees have shown, is a lot of nonsense:

We're Not That Stupid, Ignorant, or Incompetent!

The truth of the matter is that knowledge is power, and the people with the knowledge have been trying to keep it to themselves. So, when you ask how much a recommended procedure will cost, you are told not to worry about it because insurance will cover the bill. And when doctors have a choice, they have shown that they would rather not let patients see the videos by The Foundation for Informed Medical Decision Making. And if you want to check the track record of the obstetrician who just moved to your community, from two states over, you find that the information you want is not available.

Contrast this with the way the federal employees' system works. For about one month every year, employees have the option to switch polices. Therefore, the insurance companies and HMO's go courting prospective customers, sharing all the information they can about outcomes; about quality; about cost; comparing themselves with their competitors. Sounds just like a couple of competing tire stores, doesn't it?

When faced with true free-market competition, the providers don't hoard information, they share it. And for federal employees who really want to be informed, there are guidebooks published commercially that help them sort through the options for their particular circumstances. Between the advertising by providers and the guidebooks, a lot of the guesswork is taken out of the arcane field of medical insurance. Consumers have the information they need to regulate the market.

Despite the lessons there are for learning from the health system that serves our federal bureaucracy so well, the most widely discussed plan for current health care reform is something called "managed competition." Under managed competition the current system of buying health insurance from an insurance company would be shelved. Instead, employers and individuals would send money to government sponsored regional alliances which would in turn purchase health care from insurance companies and providers who would be paid on the basis of the number of people enrolled in their plan. The competition among companies would be managed by a government board that would set standard benefits and provide general oversight and management. All insurers and providers would be required to offer a standard set of benefits whether you wanted them or not. (And under some currently proposed managed competition plans, companies might not even not be free to offer enhanced benefit packages to those willing to pay more.) The managing board would also collect information on individual outcomes and would make this information available to the public through a central data base, possibly without patient authorization.

Managed competition is favored by many politicians because it does address some of the deep-rooted problems of our health care system. Most managed competition models would not allow insurers to turn away anyone, regardless of their health status, and would not allow a lifetime cap on benefits collected. It would eliminate "cherry-picking," the process by which insurance companies now compete to enroll the healthiest people by offering them lower rates while sticking those with health problems with astronomical premiums, if they can get insurance at all. It might give consumers some control by letting them judge quality and pick their own health plan. And since providers would get a set payment per person per year, it would give providers powerful (read: financial) incentive to stop ordering needless procedures and to manage their use of high-tech devices. But getting these benefits through managed competition would require creating a massive new bureaucracies that would have to engage in a fair amount of micro-managing.

Would managed competition work? As a means of solving our health care problem, probably not. The attempts to coerce insurers and providers into changing practice patterns would be met with resistance which would certainly lead to new subterfuges and abuse. But, its chief weakness is that same old bugaboo: THOSE RECEIVING THE SERVICE WOULD NOT PERCEIVE THEMSELVES AS THE PERSON PAYING THE BILL. If the system were ultimately financed through an additional annual tax collection that also paid for schools, garbage collection, socialized sewers, and everything else that government does, the relationship of payment for services rendered would get muddled. We would have created system still ripe for overuse, abuse, and traditional bureaucratic inefficiency. As one physician said to me recently, "Every time a new government program comes along, my income goes up."

One of the prime reasons cited for adopting a managed competition system of health care is that this system would reduce the options for health care to a level that the average person could handle. But the Federal Employee Health Benefit system shows that this is not necessary. GIVE THE PEOPLE THE FREEDOM TO CHOOSE THE PLAN THEY WANT AND THE MARKET WILL REGULATE ITSELF.

Before we embark on a major overhaul of our health care system, we owe it to ourselves to see if it can't work the same way everything else works in the free market. We don't need to reconstruct the whole system, to do away with insurance companies (at an estimated loss of 150,000 jobs), to establish national boards to set medical fees. We can cure much of what ails our health care system by just changing it to allow market forces to work. Put the patient in control. Give him information about quality. Give him information about cost. Give him the tax break for buying insurance. Give him the fiscal motivation to make sure he's getting the care he needs and no more. Make doctors disclose their hidden financial interests in labs and clinics so the consumer can beware when the doctor urges him to have a second course of X-rays "just to be sure." Finally, make those ancillary changes, such as reforming tort laws, that require physicians to dip into the well of defensive medicine.

How could this work in the real world? And most importantly, how would such minor changes deal with the millions of uninsured in our country?

Well, for starters, reallocating the tax benefits would come with a quid pro quo: Everyone would be required to have health insurance, just as everybody who drives is required to have car insurance. This would be acceptable under the lower costs of this new system. And the poor would still be covered under Medicaid.

Inevitably, though, there would be those who would shirk their responsibility to carry health insurance, just as some people drive without automobile insurance. Would these people be turned away from the hospital when they suddenly get sick? Of course not. They would get treatment and the hospital could send the bill to Medicaid. But then the government could recover payment through the shirker's tax return under a plan similar to the one the government is setting up to recover defaulted student loans.

Let's go back to our restaurant owner in Chapter 1. As you recall, he served four-star French cuisine to the customers and was growing richer by the day thanks to a system that let the owner bill a third party for the food. Then the system changed. People were given the means to pay their own bills. Suddenly the owner found himself being questioned about this charge and that. Why did you order the *grand cru bourgois* when a table wine was all that was necessary? Why did you have dessert sent to the table when I said I was full? Why this? Why that? Why? Why? Why? Suddenly, the restaurant owner realized that life had changed. And as he found that he had fewer customers, he began adjusting his menu and his habits. He began offering less-expensive entrees and began discussing the meals and price with customers, making sure they got what they wanted, what they needed, and nothing more. By doing this, he was able to stay comfortably in business. His colleague, who ran a four-star French restaurant in another city, refused to change with the times. He insisted on doing things the old fashioned way, and he ended up going out of business. The market had asserted itself. And the market will continue to assert itself. As Dr. John Rice, a senior physician at Duke University Arthritis Center, said recently, "Within the next 18 months almost all health care decisions will be determined by market forces."

THE FORBES SOLUTION
(An article in Forbes Magazine, *January 18, 1993)*

A year ago, like numerous other companies, we were hit with major hikes in our health insurance premiums. We responded with traditional cost-cutting measures such as boosting deductibles, but we knew that these measures alone weren't enough. They had no incentives for individuals to fundamentally change their health care habits. Our solution was to reward those who stay healthy and who avoid filing claims for routine medical expenses. Starting last January, Forbes each year offers people an opportunity to earn up to $1,000 of extra, after-tax income. Here is how it works: If someone's claims for the calendar year are under $500, we not only pay him or her the difference between that total and the $500 but we also double it; moreover, individuals will pay no payroll or income taxes. Should an employee submit medical expenses of $200, his reward would be $600 ($500-$200 = $300; $300 x 2 = $600). People here quickly recognized that each dollar of claims costs them $2 and that they win if total submissions are under $1,000 (if your expenses are $800 and you don't submit them to the insurer, you will receive that $1,000 and come out ahead by $200). Our goal was to cut down on routine, time-consuming claims and mountainous paperwork. Result: At a time when health insurance premium rates are rising an average of 20 percent or 25 percent, ours are going down almost 10 percent. Those savings will cover most of the pay-outs to our now price-conscious colleagues here. Our overall health expense increases will be a minuscule fraction of the national average. Our program has national implications in that we rely on individuals to do the job. All other approaches are top-down. They depend on bureaucrats, insurers and employers to control costs. What is so remarkable about this whole debate is the uniform assumption that individuals can't operate in this market the way they do in every other market. But you don't have to be an engineer to buy an automobile, a carpenter to buy a house or a program-

mer to purchase a computer. So, too, you don't need to be a physician to make health care choices, to seek, say, the best price for prescriptions. The U.S. doesn't have genuine free markets in health care because of the tax code. Insurance premiums are deductible for employers but not for employees. As far as individuals are concerned, health plans are almost all stick, no carrot. People should get the deductions and, if unemployed, tax credits to buy insurance. That way individuals and families could purchase insurance tailored to their own needs, not what some politico or pressure group or employer thinks they should have. Their coverage would be portable and thus not dependent on a particular job. Most individuals would opt for a big deductible, which is, in effect, what we have done here at Forbes. With free-market-oriented tax changes, tens of millions of Americans would police this market.

EPILOGUE:
IT'S AS EASY AS
ONE - TWO - THREE

If our elected officials are really serious about solving the health care crisis, there are three easy steps they can take IMMEDIATELY to reduce costs, until such time as a broader-based program can be implemented:

Step 1 - Require that in all non-emergency cases (which are 85 percent of all health care procedures) the physician discuss the costs/fees with the patient. Make the doctor look the patient in the eye and talk about how much is being charged. This simple process will cause most patients to ask real questions about quality and cost effectiveness; or, heaven forbid, who else might perform the service at a better price. Allowing the patient to understand in advance what the process really costs would be the most powerful tool available in creating efficiency and accountability in a quality/cost effective environment. This might be accomplished through a required statement of "Patients' Rights" much like the required statement of rights to persons arrested growing out of the Supreme Court's famed Miranda decision.

Step 2-Simplistically, require that each month all private and governmental employers notify their employes of the total cost being expended for health care on their behalf and receive from them a signed authorization to pay those sums for them. Better yet, although slightly more complicated would be to collect a "phantom check" from every employee each month. This check would be written by the employee for the personal pro-rata amount of the employer provided health care and workers' comp insurance coverage. The check would be destroyed upon presentation to the employer. But this simple act would become a real and constant reminder to employees of the extraordinary cost being expended for health care on their behalf. Moreover, this process would also be a reminder that the situation could change, and without efficient management by the employee, this phantom check might become a real debit in their monthly check register.

Step 3 - In order to test, and possibly eradicate the ever-present justification of defensive medicine (which ostensibly legitimizes billions of dollars in unnecessary procedures), require that every defensive procedure be coded by the provider with a big, bold **D**. Why? Think of what would be gained:

1. Physician accountability and access to statistical data. The physician becomes responsible for informing the insurance company, the patient, and society which procedures are not, in his or her professional opinion, really necessary.

2. Attorney accountability. The physician creates a stronger malpractice shield against predatory lawyers by establishing that the procedure was done specifically to avoid a lawsuit.

3. Discounted fees for defensive procedures. Society should reimburse **D** (defensive) procedures at a deeply discounted professional fee.

The logic is like this: according to physicians, what the patient really needs are the non-**D** procedures— call them the main course items. These main course procedures are supposedly those which the doctor would perform if there were no fear of a lawsuit. The physician should be paid a full professional fee for these main-course items. These full fees should cover the physician's reasonable costs and overhead and create a reasonable profit for the provider.

The defensive, or **D** procedures should be incremental to the non-**D** fees. These are performed by the provider on his own behalf only to ward off the evil trial lawyers. Since these **D** procedures are over and above what the doctor really wanted or needed to do, they are incremental and being paid in full for them represents windfall profits. Without the fee reduction for **D** procedures, the provider in essence passes along fees and costs for services performed only for his own benefit rather than that of the patient.

If the **D** code system were implemented, the result would almost certainly be a dramatic decline in the number of **D** type procedures performed, because the physician would not get a full professional fee. All procedures would become part of the regular and necessary full fee services, or they would not be performed at all. At least we would once and for all dispel the justification for defensive medicine. Quite possibly, however, we also just might eliminate a significant portion of these unnecessary procedures from our $1.0 trillion dollar health care bill.

The solutions to our health care problems do not have to be complex. There is a certain genius to the KISS principle (i.e., Keep It Simple, Stupid). Our society has been built on the ingenuity and hard work of the individual and given the opportunity, we as individuals have the ability to begin at least to solve this problem quickly, rationally and efficiently.

LISTEN TO US! We're Not That Stupid. Help us get back in control of our own health and medical destinies. That is what is best for each of us and best for the country.

SELECTED BIBLIOGRAPHY:

Altman, Lawrence K. "How tools of medicine can get in the way." *New York Times*. May 2, 1992.

Baily, Glenn W. "Litigation abuse is destroying my company," *Wall Street Journal*. July 15, 1992.

Blumstein, James F.; Perrin, James M.; and Sloan, Frank A., eds. *Cost, Quality, and Access in Health Care*. San Francisco: Jossey-Bass Publishers, 1988.

Brammer, Rhonda. "Dubious Practice? Radiation Care is at the Center of the Storm over Self Referrals," *Barrons*. March 30, 1992.

Colwell, Jack M. "Where have all the primary care applicants gone?," *New England Journal of Medicine*. February 6, 1992.

"The Crisis in Health Insurance," *Consumer Reports*. September 1990.

"Wasted Health Care Dollars,"*Consumer Reports*. July 1992.

"Health Care in Crisis: the Search for Solutions," *Consumer Reports*. September 1992.

Faltermeyer, Edward. "Let's really cure the health care system," *Fortune*. March 23, 1992.

Fein, Rashi., *Medical Care, Medical Costs. The search for a national health insurance policy*, Cambridge. Harvard College.

Goodman, John, and Musgrove, Gerald, *Patient Power*. Cato Institute. 1992.

Gordon, John Steele, "How America's Health-Care Fell Ill," *American Heritage*. May/June 1992.

Grumbach, Kevin and Lee, Philip R. "How many doctors can we afford?" *Journal of the American Medical Association*. May 8, 1991.

Ginzberg, Eli. *The limits of health reform. The search for realism*. New York: Basic Books, 1977.

Health Insurance Association of America *Source Book of Health Insurance Data 1991*. Annual Report by the HIAA. Washington D.C. 1992.

Hiatt, Howard H. et. al. "A Study of Medical Injury and Medical Malpractice," *New England Journal of Medicine*. August 17, 1989.

Horowitz, Lawrence. *Take charge of your medical fate*. New York: Random House, 1991.

Inlander, Charles B. and Moales, Karen, *Getting the most for your medical dollar*. New York: Pantheon Books, 1991.

Kemper, Vicki. "A plague on both their houses." *Common Cause*. October 1991.

Kerr, Peter. "Vast amount of fraud discovered in workers' compensation system." *New York Times*. December 29, 1991.

Lesparre, Michael, ed. *Health systems reform, then and now. 1970 and 1992.* Report of the National Health Policy Forum session at George Washington University, Washington D.C., February 19, 1992.

Long, Robert E., ed. *The crisis in health care.* New York: H.W. Wilson Co., 1991.

Marsteller, Phyllis. "A Health Insurer's Perspective: Present and Future" Speech presented to National Wellness Conference Stevens Point, Wisconsin. July 16, 1991.

Moffit, Robert E. "Surprise! A Government Health Plan That Works," *The Wall Street Journal.* April 2, 1992.

Owens, Arthur. "Earnings make a huge breakthrough," *Medical Economics.* September 3, 1990.

Reinhardt, Uwe E. *West Germany's Health Care and Health-Insurance System: Combining Universal Access with Cost Control.* Report prepared for the U.S. Bipartisan Commission on Comprehensive Health Care. Washington, D.C., August 30, 1989.

Schachner, Michael. "Benefit managers blast AMA's self-referral shift." *Business Insurance.* July 6, 1992.

Starr, Paul. *The Social Transformation of American Medicine.* New York: Basic Books, 1982.

Stevens, Robert Bocking. *Welfare Medicine in America. A Case Study of Medicaid.* New York: The Free Press, 1974.

Thornquist, Lisa. "Report to the Legislature on health care costs and cost containment in Minnesota workers compensation," Minnesota Department of Labor and Industry, Research and Education. 1990.

ABOUT THE AUTHORS

John Skvarla is President and Chief Executive Officer of Comp Containment, Inc., parent company of Isotechnologies, a leader in the development and distribution of state-of-the-art medical diagnostic equipment and a provider of physical therapy services. Mr. Skvarla was raised in Tuxedo Park, New York. He has a bachelor's degree in Economics from Manhattan College and a law degree from The University of North Carolina. Before joining Isotechnologies, he served as Chief Operating Officer of Orion Air, then the worlds largest all-cargo airline. Prior to heading Orion, Mr. Skvarla was founder and senior partner of Skvarla, Wyrick and Robbins, a law firm specializing in business and capital formation transactions.

He is a member of the Young President's Organization and an active participant of its Health Care Focus Group.

Frank Elliott is special features reporter for the *Winston-Salem Journal* where he has written widely on health care topics. In 1992 the *Journal* won the North Carolina Medical Society award for health care reporting.

ABOUT THIS BOOK

Listen to Us was composed for publication on a 486 IBM clone using Microsoft Word for Windows v.6 It was laid out on Aldus PageMaker pm4 and pm5 with great difficulty, very costly delay, and inadequate and uncooperative support from Aldus corporation technical support and customer relations. It was set at 1200 d.p.i. on a LaserMaster Truetech 1000 in postscript Book Antigua. It was printed by Thomson-Shore of Dexter, Michigan on 60 pound Thor white recycled paper using soybean ink. It was bound in Smyth sewn signatures. Four color separation for the cover was made by Image Arts of Lansing, Michigan. Book and Cover design were by Michael Brown of Chapel Hill, North Carolina. Mindy Stinner was layout and production manager. Marvin Stenhammar-Caudle of Viking Computer Services of Chapel Hill provided invaluable technical support and coordination. As always, Kinko's and UPS provided fast, reliable, and personally cooperative services.

For free rights to use any portion of the text for versions for the handicapped, write to Signal Books, P.O. Box 940, Carrboro, NC 27510. A free copy is available to adult literacy groups upon request.

Also available from
Signal Books:

Investing for Richer or Broker: Beyond the Bull
by James Veccia.

*Religion and Constitutional Government in the
United States.*
by John E. Semonche.

*Nicaragua's Continuing Revolution:
A Chronology.*
ed. David Ridenour. Signal Books and The
Center for Public Policy Research.

For a complete catalogue of our distinguished
Tidewater Fiction Series, personal narrative, and
poetry titles, write to Signal Books P.O. Box 940,
Carrborro, NC 27510. Phone (919) 929-5985. Or
Fax (919) 929-5986.